Twenty Poems

to

Nourish Your Soul

TWENTY POEMS

to

NOURISH YOUR SOUL

SELECTION AND COMMENTARY BY
JUDITH VALENTE *and* CHARLES REYNARD

LOYOLAPRESS.

CHICAGO

LOYOLAPRESS.

3441 N. ASHLAND AVENUE
CHICAGO, ILLINOIS 60657
WWW.LOYOLABOOKS.ORG

Acknowledgments and reprint permissions begin on page 211.

Cover photograph © Jack Ambrose/Getty Images
Cover and interior design by Kathryn Seckman

Library of Congress Cataloging-in-Publication Data
Twenty poems to nourish your soul / selected and introduced by Judith Valente and
Charles Reynard.
    p. cm.
  ISBN 0-8294-1869-5
  1. Spirituality. 2. Spiritual life—Christianity. 3. Christian life. 4. Religious poetry.
I. Valente, Judith. II. Reynard, Charles.
BV4501.3.T88   2005
242—dc22

                                             2005014274

Printed in the United States of America
     07 08 09 10 Versa 10 9 8 7 6 5 4 3 2

For Theresa Valente
and for
Helen Rizzoli Reynard Phoebus

Contents

༺༻

PART SIX: WORK

PART SEVEN: LOSS

PART EIGHT: BODY AND SOUL

PART NINE: MYSTERY

PART TEN: PRAYER

FOREWORD

IN A MUCH-QUOTED BUT often misunderstood line, W. H. Auden, the sage English master, states "poetry makes nothing happen": an odd thing to say for someone who spent a lifetime making poetry. Taken out of context—*In Memory of W. B. Yeats,* his homage to the great Irish poet-statesman—Auden's remark seems to suggest his art is useless in the "real" world. Indeed, he goes on to say that "executives / Would never want to tamper" with it. But then he explains that poetry persists where it originates, in

> isolation and busy griefs,
> Raw towns that we believe and die in; it survives,
> A way of happening, a mouth.

Poetry may not sway government or industry, directly anyway, but its power in the personal realm cannot be denied. During time of war or natural disaster, amid national or personal tragedy, in moments of deepest emotion—loss and anxiety, but also love and joy—it is to poetry we instinctively turn. The usual media of popular culture and mass diversion simply aren't adequate to offer the comfort, compassion, or understanding we need during life's testing and turning points. Poetry alone seems capable of expressing the most essential and profound aspects of our humanity, giving voice to what we feel but cannot easily articulate.

But crisis situations and major celebrations aside, poetry also offers, Auden notes, a "way of happening"—an approach to existing in the world, an attitude toward everyday life. We may not lead lives of "quiet desperation," as Henry David Thoreau observed. But with today's "lifestyles" we may be afflicted by noisy distraction, not to mention digital disturbances, the daily din that makes true reflection a rarity. ("I can't hear myself think!" is not just an exasperated expression.) Poetry can clear away the clutter, providing a tranquil space where *thinking,* not rote response, is possible.

In her introduction to this thoughtful and thought-provoking collection, Judith Valente notes the particular ability that poetry has to make us appreciate afresh the commonplaces of our lives, while it helps make sense of the often bewildering flux of experience. The cataclysmic events of September 11, 2001, startled a nation out of complacency and reinstilled a sense of the fragility of life, she observes. But poetry would have us give our full attention to the ordinary events that fill our days, as well, showing us what it means to be truly, fully aware of our surroundings, as is Mary Oliver in her careful concentration in *The Summer Day.*

Attentiveness, acceptance, gratitude are among the cardinal virtues that Judith Valente and her collaborator Charles Reynard discuss through the insightful poems they have chosen in this anthology. These qualities are religious, not in a narrow sectarian sense, but as spirited and spiritual ways of being in the world. The realities of work and loss, the meaning of identity, the complexity of mind-body-soul relations: these too are the substantial concerns of their selections and essays. Various as the poems and commentaries are, they share a unifying principle: a consciousness of the preciousness of life and human connections, for all the trials and disappointments.

Each of the splendid poets in the pages that follow speaks to fundamental concerns but with an individual and engaging voice, delivering the news of his or her experience and intuition in memorable language. Like all genuine poems, the works here also offer epiphanies, moments of luminous understanding to counter the routines that dull our perceptions. Great poetry, even poetry not specifically sacred, is a kind of revelation when it makes us aware of the mystery of existence itself, and the incalculable privilege we enjoy simply by *being*.

Being also implies *acting*, of course, and for thoughtful men and women that means asking serious questions about ends and means and determining what really is worth doing; in short, what to "make happen" as we try to discover how best to belong in the world. The Irish poet Eavan Boland was once asked her thoughts about the "place" of poetry in history and culture. She mentioned its visionary qualities, its ability to retrieve what might otherwise be lost, whether individual memories or the lives of the people forgotten in official accounts. She also named poets she admired who were witnesses, sometimes at the seat of power, like Yeats, but more often observing from the edge and speaking for the silenced, like Anna Ahkmatova and Adrienne Rich. At the end of their talk, the reporter asked Boland, "Do you think poetry can change the world?" The poet replied, "No, but it can change people. And that's enough."

In the poems they have chosen as well as in their personal responses to them, Judith Valente and Charles Reynard offer more than enough to think about, and a great deal to be thankful for.

Joseph Parisi

Chicago, 21 February 2005

INTRODUCTION

An UNFORGETTABLE POEM ENTERS our lives, and when it does it seizes us. It opens our spirit. It takes us to places in the self where we have never been—or that we have not yet recognized. The great Chilean poet Pablo Neruda experienced poetry in much the same way that mystics have described the relentless love of God. He writes of this experience in a poem fittingly called *Poetry:*

> . . . I don't know where
> it came from, from winter or a river.
> I don't know how or when . . .
> but from a street I was summoned,
> from the branches of night,
> abruptly from the others . . .
> and it touched me.

In an instant, poetry leads the young Neruda into the heart of a great mystery:

> And I, infinitesimal being,
> drunk with the great starry

void,
likeness, image of
mystery,
felt myself a pure part of the abyss,
I wheeled with the stars,
my heart broke loose on the wind.

Poets and lovers of poetry often speak of the moment when poetry "finds" them, opening up vistas like the one that Neruda glimpsed. Poetry found me one evening when I was ten years old. I often hid out in the bathroom, a quiet place of refuge in my family of five's small home in northern New Jersey. Evenings, I would lock the door, sit with my back against the claw-foot tub, and listen to my three-inch black transistor radio.

One night I tuned in as usual to a program on WNEW-AM New York. The disc jockey did something amazing. He read a poem on the air, something I'd never heard him do before. The poem was Edna St. Vincent Millay's *Recuerdo,* about a couple who ride back and forth all night on a ferry. I listened keenly. This was something I had done myself. I loved to take the ferry between lower Manhattan and Staten Island, and smell the tar-scented water in New York harbor, feel the moist wind on my skin, and gaze up at Manhattan's magnificent skyline.

This is what Millay put into words. When I heard her description of the sun rising, "a bucketful of gold," I thought: How can this woman know exactly what I experience riding the ferry? How can she put such precise words on my rather imprecise feeling of joy? Millay had given voice to what I could not yet speak myself. Like Neruda's, "my heart broke loose on the wind."

Poetry's power to nourish our souls is just as keen when our spirits are wounded and confused. The most dramatic recent example of this occurred in the aftermath of the terrible events of September 11, 2001. Americans turned to poetry to articulate the anguish they were feeling. Broadcasters read poetry on the air. Friends e-mailed poems to each other for comfort. The *Chicago Tribune* commissioned a poem about the attacks and published it in its news pages.

Billy Collins, who was then U.S. poet laureate, told me a few weeks after the tragedy, "At a time like this, people don't say, 'What short story should I read?' or 'What film should I go to?' But they will say, 'Do you have a poem?'"

I asked him what poems we should be reading at such a time. Collins replied: not elegies or angst-ridden lyrics, but poetry that celebrates life, the human spirit. He quoted something poet Stanley Kunitz had told an interviewer shortly after the attacks. Kunitz said he just wanted to get back to tilling his garden. In other words, to find peace and comfort in the common glories of daily life. Go to the poems. They will remind you. In times of trouble, or at *any* time for that matter. As Joseph Parisi puts it so well: "There remains poetry to remind us how we are still all too human, irreducible to the formulas of the financial markets, and capable of deeper emotions and understanding. Poetry creates meaning, a sense of the uncanny and the mystery of the universe."

At the very heart of that mystery is God.

Charles Reynard and I have selected a certain kind of poem for this book of spiritual nourishment. We concentrated mainly on modern American poets and largely avoided poems that are often anthologized in collections of religious and spiritual poetry. We did this partly to let poets of our time speak to the readers of our time. But the more important reason for this choice was to celebrate what we think is a strong *spiritual* quality in modern American poetry.

Twentieth-century American poets brought poetry down to earth. They wrote poetry, not "Poetry." They drew meaning from the everyday. "I take my poems where I find them," William Carlos Williams famously said, and he found them everywhere: in a red wheelbarrow filled with rain, in shards of green glass sticking up like grass on a hospital lot, in the damp hair he brushed from the forehead of a woman giving birth. The poets collected here, like Williams, eagerly and memorably find meaning in the commonplace.

The commonplace is also where we find God. Modern American poets may revel in this truth, but it was articulated as a spiritual principle nearly five centuries ago by St. Ignatius of Loyola. Ignatius believed that God can be found in all things—in our work as well as in our prayers, in our relationships as well as in our liturgies, in the things of our world as well as in the heavens. "The world is charged with the grandeur of God," wrote Gerard Manley Hopkins, the greatest poet to come from Ignatius's Jesuit order. In this collection, you will see poems that expose this grandeur in the ordinary. As Mary Oliver says in one of my favorite poems, *The Summer*

Day: "I don't know exactly what a prayer is. / I do know how to pay attention."

Finding God by paying attention is the theme of this collection. God isn't mentioned by name very often in these poems, but God's presence suffuses them. A mentor of mine named John Fontana once told me, "God isn't a character in our lives. God is the plot." God is in these poems—in the plot, in the details.

My coeditor and I feel a personal connection to each of these poems. Both of us live busy professional lives rooted in the "real" world. Charles Reynard is an elected Circuit Court judge in central Illinois. I am a news correspondent for PBS TV and Chicago Public Radio. Yet neither Charley nor I could imagine a single day without the lifeblood of poetry. We write poetry. We share poems late at night as we go off to sleep. We read each other poems over the phone during the workday. Poetry is not a hobby. It is part of our life's work. These twenty poems are some of our favorites, and we will tell you how they have helped us find God in all things.

We have organized the poems around ten themes rooted in Ignatian spirituality. We believe each one reflects an essential pillar for building an inner life:

- Attentiveness
- Gratitude
- Acceptance
- Simplicity
- Praise
- Work

- Loss
- Body and Soul
- Mystery
- Prayer

For each theme, we present two poems. However, as you read them you will find that many of the poems touch on several themes. The spiritual life cannot be neatly segmented; this is one concept poems articulate so well.

A short commentary accompanies each poem in which we describe how the poem has been meaningful to us. This is an invitation for you to do the same. We don't aim to tell you what the poem "means," but to suggest how you might find your own meaning. As Walt Whitman says in *Song of Myself,* "You shall no longer take things at second or third hand . . . / You shall not look through my eyes either . . . / You shall listen to all sides and filter them from your self."

We believe the poems in this anthology are not too difficult to understand. That doesn't mean they are easy. Poems have multiple meanings that unfold over time. Poetry is more intuitive than other forms of writing. It requires time and contemplation. In that sense, it shares something with prayer. Poetry contains mental leaps and emotional arcs that take effort to follow. But we are confident that this effort will be rewarded.

Poetry can be what the ancient Celts called an *anam cara,* a soul friend. It slows us down, helps us to see more deeply. It is a place of discovery. The Russian poet Yevgeny Yevtushenko imagines the poet *"right in the center / and not faltering,"* carrying his poems to the people *"as simply and calmly / as a loaf of bread."* Each of the poems in this collection has been bread for both Charles Reynard and me. Here, we offer them to you. May you find in them soul friends.

Judith Valente

PART ONE

ATTENTIVENESS

The Summer Day

Mary Oliver

Who made the world?
Who made the swan, and the black bear?
Who made the grasshopper?
This grasshopper, I mean—
the one who has flung herself out of the grass,
the one who is eating sugar out of my hand,
who is moving her jaws back and forth instead of up and down—
who is gazing around with her enormous and complicated eyes.
Now she lifts her pale forearms and thoroughly washes her face.
Now she snaps her wings open, and floats away.
I don't know exactly what a prayer is.
I do know how to pay attention, how to fall down
into the grass, how to kneel down in the grass,
how to be idle and blessed, how to stroll through the fields,
which is what I have been doing all day.
Tell me, what else should I have done?
Doesn't everything die at last, and too soon?
Tell me, what is it you plan to do
with your one wild and precious life?

THE EXAMINED LIFE
JV

MARY OLIVER IS A small, quiet-mannered woman with an unpretentious air. Quite frankly, you wouldn't notice her on a crowded street. She could be anyone's middle-aged aunt. I met her once, in October 2003, when she visited Chicago to give a reading. I probably made a fool of myself, but after the reading I rushed up to where she was signing books to tell her how her poem *The Summer Day* had changed my life. She didn't seem surprised at all. I suspect she hears that sort of thing fairly often.

Some writers describe Mary Oliver as a nature poet. I call her a mystic. Oliver lives in a place of great natural beauty, Provincetown, Massachusetts, and has spent time teaching in other scenic parts of the country, including Sweet Briar, Virginia, and Bennington, Vermont. Her poems almost always start out in the natural world, then rise, and end on a spiritual plane. In that sense, the work is both body and soul. Reading her poems, I often feel as if I've just stumbled upon a secret, one I could have uncovered on my own if only I'd looked more closely. Mary Oliver's poetry teaches me to see.

I imagine Oliver did not set out on this particular summer day to solve the philosophical inquiries, "Who made the world? Who made the swan, and the black bear?" To take the poem literally, she started out her day strolling through the fields. "What else should I have done?" I picture her at some point kneeling in the grass. She is startled by a grasshopper that leaps from the ground into her hand. Perhaps it didn't leap. Perhaps she slowly, cautiously lifted it out of the grass. At any rate, she stops. She looks. It is a moment of supreme attentiveness. One could also say of deep spirituality.

The Jesuit writer Father Anthony de Mello sees the spiritual life as a matter of "waking up":

> Most people, even though they don't know it, are asleep. They're born asleep, they live asleep, they marry in their sleep, they breed children in their sleep, they die in their sleep without ever waking up. They never understand the loveliness and the beauty of this thing that we call human existence. You know, all mystics—Catholic, Christian, non-Christian, no matter what their theology, no matter what their religion—are unanimous on one thing: that all is well, all is well. Though everything is a mess, all is well. Strange paradox, to be sure. But, tragically, most people never get to see that all is well because they are asleep. They are having a nightmare.

Oliver's examined world is complicated, mysterious, and messy. Yet it's ultimately a place of beauty and grace. In the film *American Beauty,* a teenage character named Ricky Fitts obsessively videotapes the world around him. He records even seemingly disturbing sights, such as the twisted head of a dead pigeon and the face of a frozen homeless woman.

When he tells his girlfriend the woman's face was an amazing sight, she asks, "What's amazing?" He says, "It's like God is looking right at you and if you're careful, you can look right back." Later he tries to explain why making these recordings is so important to him: "It helps me to remember—I need to remember—there is so much beauty in the world." Beauty even in the frozen stare of a dead woman.

At St. Peter's College, the director of our writing program was a devoted, demanding professor named James C. G. Conniff. He used to rant that 95 percent of his students were sleepwalking through life. How did they expect to become writers? It's a disease that affects not just students. For many years I lived the hectic life of a daily newspaper reporter. I was paid to be observant. Yet I walked to my office most days along the same streets, thoroughly absorbed in my own thoughts, oblivious to what was around me. Occasionally, I'd become vaguely aware of a building under construction on a familiar corner. Inevitably, one day something would wake me up, and I'd look over to find a gleaming new skyscraper where there had been only a hole before. I'd wonder, when did this all happen? As de Mello notes, "Waking up is unpleasant, you know. You are nice and comfortable in bed. It's irritating to be woken up."

It's interesting that Oliver doesn't ask the question, who made grasshopper*s* (plural)? Like the God who is said to count every strand of our hair, Oliver trains her eye on one specific small creature, its strange singularity. It's equally interesting that Oliver never answers her own question. Instead, she continues to observe the tiny visitor even more closely. In high school, one of my favorite teachers was Margaret Henley, who taught freshman and sophomore English. Miss Henley herself was an aspiring poet. One morning she challenged her class to recall the eye color of the bus driver who took us to school that day. The question struck me because I usually encountered the same driver on the Boulevard bus each morning, a friendly man named Sal, who often let the girls from my high school ride the bus for free. (The driver was supposed to stamp a notch on our green bus card each time we got on, but Sal would stamp the same notch over and over so we could get more rides on the same card.) I could only guess at the color of Sal's eyes. Brown, maybe?

Miss Henley asked us to memorize a short Frances Cornford poem with the unlikely title, *To a Fat Lady Seen from a Train.* I still remember these lines from the poem: "Why do you walk through the fields in gloves, / missing so much and so much?" Contrast that with Mary Oliver's willingness to touch the grasshopper with her bare hands (instead of flicking it off with a squeal of *ick,* which is probably what I'd do). It is when she stops, stoops, and examines the grasshopper that she notices its "enormous and complicated eyes"; the jaws that move "back and forth instead of up and down" in contrast to human mandibles; the rubbing of its pale forearms and that unforgettable sight: a grasshopper washing its face.

From here, the poem takes an effortless turn. The act of intensely watching this seemingly insignificant creature becomes allied in the poet's mind with an attitude of prayer. I don't think Oliver is being disingenuous when she says, "I don't know exactly what a prayer is." She's not talking about prayer encrusted in rote words, or prayer as a communal out-pouring of spirit. In Oliver's world, the worship space is an open field. One kneels to "pay attention." To be idle and atten-tive is to pray. To be idle and attentive is to be blessed.

The first time I heard *The Summer Day* read aloud, I was attending a poetry-writing workshop on Martha's Vineyard led by Marie Howe, an extraordinary poet and deeply spiritual woman who would become an important mentor. That I had summoned the courage to attend the workshop was amazing in itself. I worked for the *Wall Street Journal* then and rarely took a vacation. But somehow, brewing inside me for a num-ber of years was a sense that I should be doing another kind of writing, one by which I could tell the stories behind the jour-nalistic stories I covered for the newspaper. In other words, stories that aimed for the truth, not just the facts. I had always planned to return again to my first love, poetry. I told myself that I'd get back to it when I had more time. The truth was, I had the time. I didn't have the courage.

Applying for Marie's workshop constituted a leap of faith. I had spent years perfecting my journalistic writing. In mak-ing the switch from journalism to poetry, I felt like the con-cert pianist who suddenly decides to take up the oboe. One morning, Marie read aloud *The Summer Day.* She called it an example of a finely crafted poem. To me that morning, it was much more. The poem offered a new way of being in the world. *"Doesn't everything die at last, and too soon?"* As a teenager, I had loved the film and Broadway musical based on the novel *Zorba the Greek.* In a famous scene, Zorba tells his protégé Niko that he knew a man who "lived every minute as if he would never die." Zorba says: "I live as if I will die the next minute." Somewhere along the way, I had forgotten to live as I'd promised myself I would back then. The last lines of Oliver's poem hit me as hard as if I'd been slapped across the face. "Tell me," I asked myself, "what is it you plan to do / with your one wild and precious life?"

If Oliver merely had said, "What is it you plan to do with your precious life?" the question would have been powerful enough. But she adds, "your one *wild* and precious life." It struck me for the first time that our lives are meant to be wild and exhilarating. And that involves risk.

I was not yet ready for that kind of risk. Two more years passed before I left the *Wall Street Journal.* I might never have summoned the courage to do that if fate hadn't intervened. In November 1994, the *Journal* initiated an unprecedented layoff. One year after I had been a finalist for the Pulitzer Prize, I was laid off with fourteen other reporters. I suppose God knew I would never have the courage to leave the *Journal* on my own. So God cleared a path for me: "What is it you plan to do / with your one wild and precious life?"

I took four months off after leaving the *Journal* and went on an extended retreat. I lived during that time with the Sisters of Charity who had taught me in high school. I received several job offers from newspapers and magazines, jobs I knew would be just as demanding as the one I had left at the *Journal.* One day I found myself pacing back and forth on the street in front of the convent. I kept turning over Mary Oliver's question. I made a decision right there on the spot. I'd never again take a job so all-consuming that I'd have no time for poetry.

I decided to freelance rather than work at another traditional newspaper job. Things didn't fall into place immediately. They rarely do. It took a few years for me to hit upon the right mix of freelance work. But once I made my decision, I never gave up trying to succeed on the new path I'd chosen. Freelancing has meant I earn less money, but still enough money. Most important, it's given me the time I need to live the kind of writing life I had wanted for so long but was too afraid to give myself. The writer Joseph Campbell says that when we are truly following "our bliss," pairs of invisible hands will appear out of nowhere to help us on our way. That certainly turned out to be my experience. Periodically, I take out *The Summer Day* and reread it. It is the kind of poem that needs to be read and reread. It is a question we need to ask ourselves over and over: "what is it you plan to do / with your one wild and precious life?"

THE LAYERS
Stanley Kunitz

I have walked through many lives,
some of them my own,
and I am not who I was,
though some principle of being
abides, from which I struggle
not to stray.
When I look behind,
as I am compelled to look
before I can gather strength
to proceed on my journey,
I see the milestones dwindling
toward the horizon
and the slow fires trailing
from the abandoned camp-sites,
over which scavenger angels
wheel on heavy wings.
Oh, I have made myself a tribe
out of my true affections,
and my tribe is scattered!
How shall the heart be reconciled
to its feast of losses?
In a rising wind
the manic dust of my friends,
those who fell along the way,
bitterly stings my face.
Yet I turn, I turn,

exulting somewhat,
with my will intact to go
wherever I need to go,
and every stone on the road
precious to me.
In my darkest night,
when the moon was covered
and I roamed through wreckage,
a nimbus-clouded voice
directed me:
"Live in the layers,
not on the litter."
Though I lack the art
to decipher it,
no doubt the next chapter
in my book of transformations
is already written.
I am not done with my changes.

A MAN CALLED JOE
CR

FOR HIS ABILITY TO draw deeper meaning out of ordinary reality, Stanley Kunitz has earned the sobriquet, "a poet's poet." Approaching one hundred years old, he reigns as the unchallenged dean of contemporary American poetry. Virtually all his poems lead us to a sacred place in the heart. *Letter to My Daughters* is one of my favorites, for it never fails to remind me what a miracle it is to become a father, and what gifts my own daughters have been. It was difficult for me to single out just one Kunitz poem to include in this collection. For the universe of comforts they offer, I can commend any one of his poems to readers.

The Layers, however, is special to me because it was the first Kunitz poem I discovered. In fact, I saw only an excerpt of it that first time. It appeared on a mobile given as a gift to my dear friend Father Joe Kelly at his farewell party in 1990. It was a sad time. Joe was the priest assigned to the St. Robert Bellarmine Newman Center at Illinois State University, where my family and I regularly worshipped. Joe was being transferred from the Newman assignment to a small-town parish fifty miles west. It was not a voluntary transfer. Joe had been in campus ministry for twenty-five years. Yet he took the reassignment gracefully.

Let me tell you a little about Joe. A friend once wrote of him, "He lived a life directed at living out the Good News of the gospel message. . . . He created strong bonds with people. Some people disliked his strong opinions about issues of social justice, his out-of-the-ordinary homilies and creative liturgies. . . . Some people responded in such a way as to experience a life-changing attitude toward the gospel of discipleship." Many of us viewed the reassignment as the archbishop's retribution for Joe's independence and liberal perspective.

The priest assigned to replace Joe couldn't have been more different. He made it clear that henceforth the Newman Center would serve only students; members of the larger community, such as my family and me, could worship elsewhere. At Joe's going-away party, I learned that this poem was Joe's favorite. Only later did I discover its title. This is the excerpt that appeared on the mobile:

Oh, I have made myself a tribe
out of my true affections,
and my tribe is scattered!
How shall the heart be reconciled
to its feast of losses?

Later, when I looked up the full poem, I was struck by another set of lines: "Live in the layers, / not on the litter." What could that mean? After thinking about the lines for a long time, I began to see in them a call to wake up. A call to "live in the layers" of our lives—to peel through the litter and to discern what's most important. And then, when we have found that which is truly life affirming for us, to live in those layers, undistracted by the litter. By that time, however, Joe had already moved on. I thanked him in the silence of my heart for yet another of his gifts.

Joe had many far better friends than me. But I had no better friend than he. Our friendship was never truer than in the fall of 1996 when I was running for my third term as state's attorney of McLean County, Illinois. Stupidly, I had gotten into a fistfight with my much younger opponent after a particularly heated debate in which he called me a number of less-than-flattering names. When this happened, Joe had been gone for quite a while. As soon as he learned of the incident, he drove to see me. We met in the living room of the Catholic Worker home not far from the Newman Center.

He didn't lecture me. He didn't say anything at first. He simply listened to my story. Then he encouraged me to take heart. I'd made a mistake. I needed to ask for forgiveness, and then forgive myself. He wasn't wearing any priestly garb, but I recognize now that he had offered me the sacrament of reconciliation. "In my darkest night, / when the moon was covered / . . . I roamed through wreckage." Though he didn't say it then, Joe was exhorting me to "live in the layers, / not on the litter." He gave me the strength of heart to recognize I could and would do better in the future.

Joe once gave a homily about friendship that I have never forgotten. I heard it just a year or two after I began attending the Newman Center following many years of disaffection with the Catholicism of my youth. It was a Sunday after Easter, and Joe spoke about the meaning of the Resurrection in our lives today. The Resurrection, he said, is meant to "bring the power of faith and new life to every part of our living, to very ordinary and common human activity." His friends found a copy of the homily among his notes after his death. He called it "Friendship As Sacrament":

> A lot of energy can go into fulfilling the requirements of our Christian faith so that we can feel and claim a love for God in heaven. But there is no risk in such loving. We have to take risks to love each other, to give ourselves to others, then receive from others the trust they place in us. Human friendship is at the core of our Christian faith. Human friendship is opening ourselves to the spirit of the Resurrection and giving it human flesh, making it real in the human family here and now. We all have friends. Although each of those friendships has a distance to go for further growth, already it is those friendships that have given our lives meaning and made God's love real to us, that have made the power of Resurrection shatter the tombs of painful isolation and aloneness. Realize and appreciate those friendships.

Behind Kunitz's poem is a similar wisdom. How are we to live in the layers during our darkest nights of isolation and loneliness? How are we to appreciate that "every stone on the road" is precious when our sight is obscured by pain and regret? One way we do it is through the support of our "sacramental" friends, those who recognize that there is meaning in our life's layers.

In the spring of 1998, Joe was dying of lung cancer. Not surprisingly, he chose to live out his final vigil not in a rectory surrounded by other priests or in a hospice center but at Clare House, a facility that serves the poor. Two women friends from the old Newman Center group visited him with a gift from our community. It was a quilt of many squares recalling the memories of our lives with him. They found him reclining on a daybed. His breathing was labored, but he smiled gently as he rubbed the quilt between his fingers. His eyes seemed to moisten with his own memories of his Newman Center friends. He had lost his strength to the cancer, but not his dry, self-effacing humor. At one point he gazed at the women and held up the quilt. Then with a furrowed brow, a mocking sarcasm in his voice, he asked, "Is that all?" He was preparing for the most profound transformation, death. Yet he could still launch a joke. "I turn, I turn, / exulting somewhat, / with my will intact to go / wherever I need to go, / and every stone on the road / precious to me." He was not done with his changes.

I recently came across the final homily Joe gave to the Newman community in August 1990. It was printed in a book of his homilies collected by a group of his Newman friends. He referred obliquely that day to Kunitz's poem, and noted that there are many ways to view the past. "For our purposes, a significant way is to observe 'two layers of life': one, the events of history, and the second, the reaction to those events by people of faith." He recalled the Holocaust and a woman who remembered how her mother risked her life to hide Jewish children. The mother explained to her daughter, "It's the Christian thing to do."

To this day, I hear Joe's "nimbus-clouded voice" exhorting me to live in the layers. It is something I think about daily as I step up to my chair on the judicial bench and try to discern truth from fact and eke out some measure of justice for people who may have tasted little of it in our flawed world. I have thought many times of the lines I first saw on his mobile. "I have made myself a tribe / out of my true affections, / and my tribe is scattered!" I could not have known then how much my life was to change after his death, and how much more those words would come to mean to me. Two years after Joe died, my wife and I separated and subsequently divorced. Although we ultimately decided we were better and stronger people apart than together, the divorce represented a devastating failure for us both. It caused immeasurable pain for our two daughters, which was perhaps the hardest pain to bear.

Many nights I found myself pondering the words from the mobile, "How shall the heart be reconciled / to its feast of losses?" With time and a great deal of effort, we have all started to heal. I have come to accept that while my marriage failed, the love my wife and I once shared did not. It manifests itself every day in our two daughters and in the way they have grown into bright, talented, caring young women. I have learned to forgive myself as Joe taught me to do in that living room so many years ago. Like Kunitz, I can look back on my past, and say,

> I have walked through many lives,
> some of them my own,
> and I am not who I was,

though some principle of being
abides . . .

With the example of my dear friend Father Joe Kelly as a guiding light, I can look to the future, and whatever challenges it brings, with confidence and hope. Dear Joe, "I am not done with my changes."

PART TWO

GRATITUDE

ALIVE TOGETHER

Lisel Mueller

Speaking of marvels, I am alive
together with you, when I might have been
alive with anyone under the sun,
when I might have been Abélard's woman
or the whore of a Renaissance pope
or a peasant wife with not enough food
and not enough love, with my children
dead of the plague. I might have slept
in an alcove next to the man
with the golden nose, who poked it
into the business of stars,
or sewn a starry flag
for a general with wooden teeth.
I might have been the exemplary Pocahontas
or a woman without a name
weeping in Master's bed
for my husband, exchanged for a mule,
my daughter, lost in a drunken bet.
I might have been stretched on a totem pole
to appease a vindictive god
or left, a useless girl-child,
to die on a cliff. I like to think
I might have been Mary Shelley
in love with a wrongheaded angel,
or Mary's friend. I might have been you.
This poem is endless, the odds against us are endless,

our chances of being alive together
statistically nonexistent;
still we have made it, alive in a time
when rationalists in square hats
and hatless Jehovah's Witnesses
agree it is almost over,
alive with our lively children
who—but for endless ifs—
might have missed out on being alive
together with marvels and follies
and longings and lies and wishes
and error and humor and mercy
and journeys and voices and faces
and colors and summers and mornings
and knowledge and tears and chance.

Speaking of Marvels
IV

Now in her eighties, Lisel Mueller is still a trim, spry woman. Impeccably dressed, her ash-colored hair cut pixie style, she looks out at the world with intense blue eyes. Mueller left her native Germany when she was a teen, but still exudes an old-world charm. Her one-bedroom apartment on Chicago's north side, like the woman who inhabits it, is subtle and modest. A coffeemaker sits on the kitchen counter. Odd pieces of notepaper litter her writing desk. Pictures of family decorate one wall. One item stands out. Sitting atop a Plexiglas case in the living room is a small, five-sided glass object containing the profile of a man: the Pulitzer Prize she won in 1997 for poetry.

The same combination of subtlety and style one finds in her home pervades Lisel Mueller's work. I spent a day with her in the fall of 2003 for a report I did on Chicago Public Radio. Lisel's eyesight has faded to a blur over the years because of severe glaucoma. Though she can still make out faces and discern objects up close, she can no longer read without the help of a magnifying machine that resembles an overhead projector. At her now-rare public readings, she recites her poems from memory, though she occasionally glances down at the page to give the appearance of reading. Her husband of fifty-eight years died in 2001. His death robbed her of a trusted reader, a tireless supporter of her work, and her best friend. Yet when she talked about her life, it wasn't the deficits she dwelled on. She spoke of those almost matter-of-factly. Of all the poems Lisel recited for me from memory that day, she delighted in none more than *Alive Together,* the poem she chose as the title of her Pulitzer Prize-winning *New and Selected Poems.* She called it her "happiness poem."

"It suddenly came to me in a flash, as things do, what a wonderful life I had, and if I hadn't been the person I am genetically and hadn't come to the United States and hadn't met my husband, everything would have been different. So it's about the fact that we could have been anyone. That's what the poem says, we could have been anyone in history—geographically different, genetically different. It's just such a matter of chance to be who you are and live the life you've been given."

The poem is in many ways a classic list poem. It begins with these amazing first lines:

> Speaking of marvels, I am alive
> together with you, when I might have been
> alive with anyone under the sun.

The poem then moves through a litany of "might have beens." The poet might have been born a slave in nineteenth-century America. Or a girl-child in a culture where parents abandon female babies. She might have been Mary Shelley. She might have been you. As she points out, the possibilities are endless. The poem is endless.

I once watched a film on how life begins. It struck me for the first time how mysterious and downright complex it is to create a human life. In the process of conception, literally millions of sperm are released. Only a few hundred survive the arduous journey through the female reproductive tract. Only one will ultimately join with the female's ovum. That event must take place within a twenty-four–hour window. Then consider all the circumstances that must align to bring two people together in the same room. Add to that all the emotional cards that have to fall into place so the same two people can fall in love. My parents met in evening high school when my father happened to walk by the open door to the classroom where my mother was sitting. They encountered each other because their parents—from three different towns in Italy—all found themselves alive together at the same time in the same American city. When we think of all the chance and choice that must conspire to bring us into the world, it's amazing we come to exist at all! As the poem points out:

The odds against us are endless,
our chances of being alive together
statistically nonexistent;
still we have made it.

The members of our family form the basic fabric of our lives, but the people we meet along the way, for good or for ill, fill out the rest of that tapestry. I felt that very deeply once as I sat in a pew at St. Peter's Basilica in Rome, waiting for Christmas Eve Midnight Mass to begin. I had come to Italy with a few of my closest friends to celebrate the millennium. As luck would have it, we were able to acquire tickets to sit inside St. Peter's. We arrived several hours early to get the best seats we could. My mind wandered in a hundred different directions as I waited for the service to begin. I decided to pass the time saying a short prayer for all the people who had impacted my life. I thought first of my parents, Charles and Theresa Valente. Then the Sisters of Charity who had taught me in high school: Sister Lorraine Casella, now deceased, who encouraged me to be a writer; Sister Helen Jean Everett, the Latin teacher, who infused in all her students a love for language and the humanities; Sister Mary Alexandrine, the school treasurer, who befriended me my freshman year when, as a transfer from a public school, I didn't have many friends among the students. I thought of Duncan Henderson, the Presbyterian elder who had cared for his son dying of AIDS, and whose story I had chronicled on the front page of the *Wall Street Journal*. That story would become a Pulitzer Prize finalist.

What took me completely by surprise was that I soon found myself giving thanks for people I hadn't previously considered constructive in my life, such as the bureau chief I had worked for in London. When I joined the London bureau of the *Wall Street Journal,* I was at the peak of my career and had recently been nominated for a Pulitzer. My London editor seemed to expect perfection of me. When he didn't get it, he quickly soured on my work and on my story ideas. His attitude wore away at my confidence to the point that I began to question whether my writing talent had simply disappeared.

When the *Journal* had a layoff in my second year in London, my name showed up on the list. It was a terrible shock to lose my job. Yet, if it hadn't been for that dreadful, soul-shaking experience in London, I might still be toiling away at the *Journal* instead of doing the kind of writing I'm doing now, the writing I was meant to do all along. For that, I can feel only gratitude.

Not long ago, I attended a women's retreat in central Illinois. On our last afternoon together, we gathered outside on the wide porch of the retreat house. It was a fresh, summer-like day in mid-April. The retreat leader asked each person to write, anonymously, on a slip of paper a question or a problem she was struggling with and would like to draw upon the collective wisdom of the group to resolve. The slips of paper went into a basket. One by one, we pulled them out and read them aloud. One woman wrote:

> All of my life I have struggled with the feeling that I am unlovable, that I am not worthy of love. Even when I have been in a relationship, this feeling creeps in and inevitably ruins the relationship. What can I do to believe once and for all that I am worthy of love?

The question drew a hushed response. I sensed a collective aching for this woman. Yet how could anyone answer her question? Much to my surprise, I heard myself say, "I'd like to answer that." I still don't know where these words came from. I said, "All of us have gotten to where we are because of love. Someone, somewhere along the line loved you, or else you wouldn't have survived. Maybe there was more than one person who at some point showed you some form of love. Think of those people every day. Those experiences say you are worthy of love. Build on them a little each day. One day, you too will begin to see how worthy you are."

I can only hope that the author of that note took those words to heart and that they were of some small comfort. I was grateful to be alive together at that moment with that woman.

As often as I've read *Alive Together*, a different line seems to jump out at me each time and reveal new meaning. Recently it was "Still we have made it." I had just come back from teaching a poetry workshop with Charley at the Cook County Juvenile Detention Center. Charley and I go there once a month under the auspices of the chaplain's office. Crystal is one of the teen-age girls incarcerated at the facility. That day's workshop focused on metaphor. We asked the students to write a poem beginning with the words, "My life is . . ." Crystal handed in this poem, reprinted here exactly as written:

My Life

I was just a little
girl when I started
raising my little sisters
and little brother
one day walking
from school a black man
about six feet tall jumped
out and grab me, took

me into dark alley and
and raped me at the
age of 12 years old I felt
that my hole life was
taken from me no one
shoulder to cry on
no one to
	lean on
no mother to run to
it was just lonely in my
	life.

The poem is devastating to read. At first it filled me with hopelessness for this young girl. How could she ever overcome such deep wounds inflicted so early in life? Then I thought of Father Dave Kelly and Father Denny Kinderman, the two chaplains who visit the detention center every day. They never fail to tell these teenagers they are happy to see them. They talk about things the kids want to talk about. When I read Crystal's poem now, I take comfort in the fact that she has Father Dave and Father Denny to support her, and that she had the strength to write that poem. She can honestly say, "still we have made it."

"But for endless ifs," the poem says, our lives might have been very different. These days, when Lisel Mueller talks about *Alive Together,* the conversation inevitably turns to her late husband. With glee she relates how they both met in college in Indiana. She was a refugee from Nazi Germany. One day as she studied alone in an empty classroom, Paul Mueller walked in. He had taken a job washing classroom windows to earn tuition money. Paul was a music major, and he hummed a beautiful melody as he worked. When Lisel asked him what it was, he told her it was Franck's symphony. "I understood him to say 'Brahms's,' and so I said, 'Oh, which symphony?' And he said, rather haughtily, 'Well, Franck only wrote one.'"

It was a funny way to fall in love! They married when both were nineteen and he was about to enter the army in World War II. Lisel credits her husband with giving her the kind of support and space she needed for her writing. "He was always willing to watch the children when I went out of town for readings. He was at the airport to pick me up when I came back. There was always a pot of coffee ready for me when I came home." Lisel told me she has been unable to write any new poems since her husband died. But *Alive Together* remains as an expression of gratitude for those years they had together. It is the poem that more than any other brought me together with the man I share my life with, who I wouldn't have met . . . "but for endless ifs."

My engagement to someone else had broken up some seven months before. Meeting someone new was the farthest thing from my mind. In fact, I was ready to remain an independent, fulfilled single person for the rest of my life. Then my friend Kathleen Kirk invited me to attend a women's retreat at her church in Normal, Illinois. The retreat would take place on a weekend in April 2002. I checked my calendar and had commitments every weekend that month—except that weekend. Kathleen was teaching a poetry-writing workshop at the Normal library, and, by coincidence, her students were scheduled to give a reading the day after our retreat ended. Kathleen asked me if I could stay an extra day and read some of my poems.

One of the students in her workshop was the state's attorney of her county. He had recently been elected a Circuit Court judge but hadn't been sworn in yet. Kathleen also had invited another of our mutual friends to the reading, a woman who had given up the practice of law to write poetry. She thought this woman might make a good match for the newly elected judge. When the reading was over, Kathleen invited both of them to go out with her for a bite to eat. I went along as a fourth wheel. The new judge turned out to be Charles Reynard. We ended up seated across from each other in the restaurant, and again at Kathleen's kitchen table when we went back to her house to chat. I had been reading Lisel's *Alive Together* collection and read the poem aloud at the kitchen table. I could tell Charley was deeply moved. I happened to mention that I had an extra ticket to an upcoming reading the poet was giving in Chicago. Kathleen said she wasn't free to go that night. Neither was our other friend. Finally, Kathleen said jokingly, "Charley, would you like to go with Judy?" He said he would, to everyone's surprise, I think.

Lisel read *Alive Together* that night at the reading. It was as if she was reading expressly to the two of us. We went out to dinner that night and shared some of our own poems with each other. I was impressed at how this prosecutor, soon to be a judge, revealed so much of his own vulnerability in his poems. We were both at critical stages in our lives. My mother had died a few months before, and Charley, who had been very close to his mother, seemed to really understand the intense grief I was feeling. His marriage had broken up a few years before. He understood the sense of loss and failure that follows even when we know the breakup is for the best. Since that night at Lisel Mueller's reading, *Alive Together* has become "our poem." It reminds us of how acutely blessed we are to have met—two people, he in his fifties, I in my forties— finding, at our ages, a second chance at love. The odds of this inveterate city dweller falling in love with a man from small-town central Illinois seem quite to defy the odds. Still we are here, grateful to be "alive / together with marvels and follies / and longings and lies and wishes / and error and humor and mercy / and journeys and voices and faces / . . . and knowledge and tears and chance."

WHAT THE LIVING DO
Marie Howe

Johnny, the kitchen sink has been clogged for days, some
    utensil probably fell down there.
And the Drano won't work but smells dangerous, and the
    crusty dishes have piled up

waiting for the plumber I still haven't called. This is the
    everyday we spoke of.
It's winter again: the sky's a deep headstrong blue, and the
    sunlight pours through

the open living room windows because the heat's on too high
    in here, and I can't turn it off.
For weeks now, driving, or dropping a bag of groceries in the
    street, the bag breaking,

I've been thinking: This is what the living do. And yesterday,
    hurrying along those
wobbly bricks in the Cambridge sidewalk, spilling my coffee
    down my wrist and sleeve,

I thought it again, and again later, when buying a hairbrush:
    This is it.
Parking. Slamming the car door shut in the cold. What you
    called *that yearning.*

What you finally gave up. We want the spring to come and
    the winter to pass. We want
whoever to call or not call, a letter, a kiss—we want more and
    more and then more of it.

But there are moments, walking, when I catch a glimpse of
    myself in the window glass,
say, the window of the corner video store, and I'm gripped by
    a cherishing so deep

for my own blowing hair, chapped face, and unbuttoned coat
    that I'm speechless:

I am living, I remember you.

A CHERISHING SO DEEP

JV

THERE ARE PEOPLE YOU meet who leave an indelible impression from the very first. Marie Howe is one of those people. I first met Marie when she was leading a poetry workshop on Martha's Vineyard in July 1992. It was the first poetry workshop I'd ever signed up for, a tentative step to get back to the writing that had always been my first love. Meeting Marie was one of those "odds against us" set of circumstances Lisel Mueller describes in *Alive Together*. A friend and I had thumbed through a book on poetry workshops across the country. We happened upon the entry for the Martha's Vineyard workshop. "Let's go there," I said without giving it much thought. That was the extent of my research. I had never even seen Marie's work.

Marie is a strikingly tall woman with long, flowing hair. She seemed so self-assured, I felt shy around her at first. Then Marie did something totally unexpected. She picked up my suitcase and carried it up two flights of stairs to my room. That first evening, Marie read her poems to the group. Her younger brother John had recently died of AIDS. For her second collection she was working on a series of poems about his illness and death. The poems were so achingly honest, I felt as though I had peered into Marie's soul. I went back to my room that night with her poems replaying in my head. I thought, if I have to spend the rest of my life trying, I want to be able to write like that, I want my words to be able to touch people that deeply.

I had just finished writing a long piece for the *Wall Street Journal* about Duncan Henderson, a Midwestern father and devout Presbyterian, who cared for his son, Paul, the entire time Paul was dying of AIDS. I had never seen anyone waste away so insidiously of a disease. Marie's poems—the raw emotion and accuracy of details she put into them—closely mirrored my own experience with Paul. In one poem, for instance, she describes how her brother laid out his array of medications by numbers in an egg carton, "so there'd be no mistake." Of all the poems Marie read that night, none struck me more than *What the Living Do*. At the workshop, I had showed her a poem of mine, addressed to Paul as he slipped further away in the last days of his life. Marie said, "But you're telling him things he already knows. What about talking to him about the things he can't know?"

What the Living Do is addressed to her brother, weeks after his death. It begins by detailing a particular morning, one which a person in a different frame of mind could easily dismiss as a bad day. The kitchen sink is clogged, and Drano isn't helping. The dishes are piling up. It's cold outside, but the heat in the apartment is cranked up too high. The dead forfeit just such moments: driving a car, carrying a bag of groceries in the street, dropping the bag, spilling coffee, buying a hairbrush. How different all of those seemingly insignificant acts would look if we knew we would never get a chance to do them again. As Marie says,

> This is it.
> Parking. Slamming the car door shut in the cold. What
>   you called *that yearning*.
>
> What you finally gave up.

We often hear self-help gurus talk about "living in the moment." And it's true we don't appreciate "what is" nearly enough. We find ourselves absorbed in what we don't have, what could be different, better. So often when I get on the elevator in my building, people are talking about the weather. In winter, someone inevitably complains about how cold it is. Come July, the same people say, "When is this heat going to end?"

> . . . We want the spring to come and the winter to pass.
>   We want
> whoever to call or not call, a letter, a kiss—we want more
>   and more and then more of it.

Marie often told her students, "Run your hand over the page you've written. Where's the real heat of the poem?" For me, the real heat in *What the Living Do* comes in the last seven lines. In that moment, the poet feels intense gratitude for the simple ability to walk down a street, to catch a glimpse of herself reflected in a shop window. It creates in her "a cherishing so deep." It is a cherishing of her own windblown hair, chapped face, unbuttoned jacket. The experience is so profound that it leaves her speechless. I thought again about Paul Henderson. He was forty-three years old, a short life by today's standards. He died full of regret. One day, he told me sadly that he had wasted so much time being depressed. I never forgot that. But I also know I didn't take the lesson nearly enough to heart. Too often, I gave into feelings of depression when things didn't go perfectly in my life. It was only when my mother died suddenly of a stroke in 2001 that I began to understand more fully the kind of cherishing Marie meant. Perhaps I needed the wake-up call of someone close to me dying.

My mother was such an integral part of my life, it seemed preposterous to me that she could be gone from it forever. Her death showed me just how vulnerable I am. I realized in ways I never had before, that I too am going to die one day. I remember how my mother, when she entered her eighties, would rise before dawn to see the beginning of a new day. She always felt grateful for having lasted another night. She prayed for about two hours every morning. Her first prayer was always one of thanksgiving. After she died, I found myself waking earlier, too, trying to catch a glimpse of the sunrise. I felt privileged now to see the sun come up. It was a privilege my mother no longer enjoyed. Sometimes this cherishing would strike me in the oddest places. I remember going into a deli and ordering a corned beef sandwich. I suddenly burst into tears right there at the table at the sight of slices of corned beef lying on a bed of pumpernickel. I thought of how my mother loved corned beef and pastrami sandwiches. When I was in college, we would mark the start of a new semester by shopping in New York, then stopping by the Carving Board restaurant at Macy's for a sandwich. I felt horrible that my mother could no longer have this pleasure. I felt guilty that I could. Then it occurred to me that one way of cherishing those memories is to go to a deli every once in a while and order a corned beef or pastrami sandwich, to give thanks for those memories, and in so doing, honor my mother. It is a way of saying, "I am living. I remember you."

Marie taught me another valuable lesson about gratitude. It was a lesson that actually came in two parts, separated by about nine years. In 1992, when the Martha's Vineyard workshop was over, Marie offered me a ride to Boston, where I was to catch my plane back to Chicago. By then I had read her first collection, *The Good Thief.* It was obvious from the poems that Marie's family life had been difficult. Her relationship with her father was particularly flawed. Poetry is a form of healing, she pointed out. "The wounded have to become the healers." In 2001, I attended another workshop Marie led, in Spoleto, Italy. She asked the class to try writing a "praise poem," a poem that pays homage to someone or something. As a model, she read her poem, *The Attic.* In it, Marie chillingly recounts her father stumbling up to her room in the attic and the sound of his weight on the springs of her bed. She does not describe what happens next. One can imagine. Marie said she had wanted to write about these painful episodes of her life, but couldn't seem to do it without the poem sounding like a therapy exercise. She decided to try to find something affirming about the whole rotten experience. That's when she remembered her older brother. *The Attic* begins:

> Praise to my older brother, the seventeen-year-old boy, who lived
> in the attic with me an exiled prince . . .

The poem ends with a description of the brother rising from the chair at his drafting-room table, where he is designing an imaginary building. When he hears his father stumble back down the stairs, he knocks on his sister's door, sits down, and draws his arms around his sister:

> I don't know if he knows he's building a world where I can one day
> love a man—he sits there without saying anything.

> Praise him.
> I know he can hardly bear to touch me.

By choosing to focus on that small act of compassion, Marie gives power to those parts of her troubled past that were life-giving. In that way, life declares victory over the forces that would suffocate it. In short, a matter for praise.

A few years ago, I began doing nightly what St. Ignatius of Loyola called the *examen*. It is a daily accounting of what I did well each day and of where I fell short. I also list all that happened that I'm grateful for. It's my favorite part of the *examen*. The funny thing about gratitude is, the more you focus on it, the more you find to be grateful for. These days, I find myself more and more grateful for the most ordinary of moments—when I look out on the ever-changing prairie as I drive each week from Chicago to Charley's and my home in central Illinois. As I walk past our living-room windows in the middle of the day and spot the sunlight sifting in through a latticework of branches. In those moments, I stop and remember how grateful I am to be alive. In the final scene of the film *American Beauty*, the main character, Lester Burnham, speaking from the grave, says he doesn't feel regret that he's no longer alive, only intense gratitude "for every single moment of my stupid little life." Then he adds: "You have no idea what I'm talking about, I'm sure. But don't worry, someday you will."

PART THREE

ACCEPTANCE

The God Who Loves You
Carl Dennis

It must be troubling for the god who loves you
To ponder how much happier you'd be today
Had you been able to glimpse your many futures.
It must be painful for him to watch you on Friday evenings
Driving home from the office, content with your week—
Three fine houses sold to deserving families—
Knowing as he does exactly what would have happened
Had you gone to your second choice for college,
Knowing the roommate you'd have been allotted
Whose ardent opinions on painting and music
Would have kindled in you a lifelong passion.
A life thirty points above the life you're living
On any scale of satisfaction. And every point
A thorn in the side of the god who loves you.
You don't want that, a large-souled man like you
Who tries to withhold from your wife the day's disappointments
So she can save her empathy for the children.
And would you want this god to compare your wife
With the woman you were destined to meet on the other campus?
It hurts you to think of him ranking the conversation
You'd have enjoyed over there higher in insight
Than the conversation you're used to.
And think how this loving god would feel
Knowing that the man next in line for your wife
Would have pleased her more than you ever will
Even on your best days, when you really try.

Can you sleep at night believing a god like that
Is pacing his cloudy bedroom, harassed by alternatives
You're spared by ignorance? The difference between what is
And what could have been will remain alive for him
Even after you cease existing, after you catch a chill
Running out in the snow for the morning paper,
Losing eleven years that the god who loves you
Will feel compelled to imagine scene by scene
Unless you come to the rescue by imagining him
No wiser than you are, no god at all, only a friend
No closer than the actual friend you made at college,
The one you haven't written in months. Sit down tonight
And write him about the life you can talk about
With a claim to authority, the life you've witnessed,
Which for all you know is the life you've chosen.

God Is the Plot
CR

JUDY AND I HAVE enjoyed many a spirited discussion over our beliefs. Carl Dennis's poem *The God Who Loves You* has sparked some of the most lively of those discussions. Judy was born and raised as a traditional Catholic, while I wasn't baptized until age seven, and then only because a new best friend in a new neighborhood attended St. Joan of Arc parochial school, and I wanted to be like him. (I'm only half joking when I call Catholicism the religion of friendship.) My struggles with Catholic doctrine and with a range of faith issues began not too many years after the rather secular origin of my conversion.

The God Who Loves You zooms in on one of my more enduring struggles: if God plays an ongoing role in creation, how do we reconcile those parts of our lives and our world that are messy, flawed, unjust, even tragic? How do we come around to acceptance of our world and of ourselves?

Those questions challenge our traditional image of God. We often envision God as a chess master, moving humans around like so many rooks and pawns on a board. Or, we imagine God as a kind of professional advance man who runs around pulling together meetings and events, causing people to meet, or not. All we mere mortals have to do is show up for life. The rest is taken care of.

Here in the Western world, we have developed a photographic image of God. Though God never sat for portraiture as far as we can tell, we just *know* he's a lot like the white-haired man with the long beard in Michelangelo's painting, extending his finger outward to infuse Adam with life. Holding to that image, it's easy to give God all the credit when things go right. But what are we to think when we receive news of that devastating diagnosis, when we lose a job unfairly through a layoff, or when we suffer the sudden loss of a loved one?

As a journalist, Judy once interviewed people of faith whose relatives died in the 1995 Oklahoma City bombing. How had they coped with the tragedy? How had it affected their faith? Could they find it in their hearts to forgive the bomber? One woman, whose husband was killed, recounted an interesting story. The father of one young woman credited his daughter's survival in the attack to the fact that he prayed for her every morning right around the time she reported to work. The woman who'd lost her husband tearfully asked Judy: "Did that mean the people whose loved ones had died didn't pray for them, or didn't pray hard enough?"

One evening a few days before Thanksgiving, a neighbor of ours stood in our kitchen and related to us how he had lost his faith in God. He said that when he was quite small, his father developed cancer. "My brother and I were told to pray for my father so he would get better. But he died. I stopped believing in God that very day." What could we say to him? There isn't an easy answer for why his prayers weren't answered, why his young father had to suffer cancer in the first place. This may strike against the grain of what so many believe, but I don't think of God as a producer, director, orchestrator, or even as a stage manager. I do believe that God is present. God is there in the unfolding plot.

The God in Carl Dennis's poem isn't some grand puppeteer. In Dennis's world, we are not so much at the mercy of God's detailed plan for us as we are the victims or benefactors of our individual choices. This is a God who frets over the other lives we might have lived had we chosen them. What if we had gone away to college and not stayed home? What if we had chosen a different spouse, the one we would have met had we gone to that other college? Dennis's God even calculates how many years we shaved off our life expectancy by our own stupidity, like running out in the snow without a coat to fetch the morning paper.

Within the poem is another struggle, the one for self-acceptance. I have waged that battle my entire life. Without saying so directly, Dennis challenges us to accept the divine within—literally infused with the life we've "witnessed," as he puts it, the life we've been given. The poem reminds me that as long as I regard God as outside of me, I am destined to wonder endlessly about my own worthiness, my own guilt. I am fated to question whether, with a little more fidelity, skill, or luck, with a little more time to bargain, I might have become more acceptable, more lovable, more worthy. But if I recognize that God is in me and in others, rather than separate and apart, how can I not then accept myself, my life, and others as they are?

The poem also reminds me that each day I am creating my life by the choices I make. In that sense, I bear a sobering responsibility. I suspect that some of us prefer the notion of God as CEO, the big guy in the front office who calls the shots. We might even find that image comforting. I like what the philosopher and writer Miguel de Unamuno once said about belief: "Those who believe that they believe in God, but without passion in their hearts, without anguish in mind, without uncertainty, without doubt, without an element of despair, can in their consolation believe only in the God idea, not God himself." By owning our responsibility, we actually become more free, not less. I am now more conscious of the choices I make. I try to think of their consequences *before* I act. This is not to say that prayer is futile, or that it's inappropriate to ask for God's guidance. But to me, there is a difference between seeking a particular outcome from God, and what I like to think of as leaning into the mystery of life, letting life unfold. What transpires ultimately may be the outcome we sought. It may be much different, or perhaps much better. We just might find that the life we know is the life we would have chosen.

To the Mistakes
W. S. Merwin

You are the ones who
were not recognized
in time although you
may have been waiting
in full sight in broad
day from the first step
that set out toward you
and although you may
have been prophesied
hung round with warnings
had your big pictures
in all the papers
yet in the flesh you
did not look like that
each of you in turn
seemed like no one else
you are the ones who
are really my own
never will leave me
forever after
or ever belong
to anyone else
you are the ones
I must have needed
the ones who led me

in spite of all that
was said about you
placing my footsteps
on the only way

PAZIENZA
CR

W. S. MERWIN OFTEN addresses himself to unusual listeners in his poems: *To the Light of September, To the Fire, To a Few Cherries, To Prose,* and *To the Dust of the Road.* In this poem, he speaks to his mistakes. Perhaps it is only Merwin's imagined narrator speaking. I prefer to think it is the poet himself, who rises in humility to the challenge of accepting himself.

There is, in Merwin's poem, a connection to Carl Dennis's *The God Who Loves You.* Dennis invites his readers to embrace their status with grace, and to shed the burden of second-guessing the narrative twists of their lives. Dennis asks us to accept our choices. Merwin drives the logic of this challenge even further. He dares us to accept our mistakes. Ordinarily, we regard our mistakes as bad, as meriting regret. Merwin believes they are as integral to our lives as our successes. They are essential parts of ourselves. They "are the ones who / are really my own / never will leave me / forever after / or ever belong / to anyone else."

I don't believe Merwin is talking about the difficult or traumatic events that can befall any human being—an accident, an illness, or a layoff. He is talking about the mistakes we provoke. He points out something so true: our mistakes often stare us right in the face before we make them, though we are too dim to notice. They "may have been waiting / in full sight in broad / day from the first step / that set out toward you." These are the errors and bad judgments that make us feel stupid and worthless. Merwin realizes that many of his mistakes didn't materialize out of thin air. Some of them were "hung round with warnings / had [their] big pictures / in all the papers." They are the mistakes that, depending on the consequences, leave permanent, exquisitely sensitive scars upon us, and probably upon others as well.

The poet proposes a difficult exercise: to confront the truly serious mistakes that have marked us in profound ways. It is not emotionally convenient to think about these mistakes, much less to own them. But only by doing so, Merwin seems to be saying, can we feel the first stirrings of wisdom. While you are summoning the courage to do this exercise (out loud, if at all possible, and to someone else, maybe a very particular someone else), I will recount one of my biggest mistakes and most bitter humiliation—the kind that produced "big pictures / in all the papers."

On November 16, 1995, I had been state's attorney, the chief prosecuting authority and legal officer of McLean County, Illinois, for just under nine years. I was in the first month of a heated reelection campaign. I was fifty years old, a husband for twenty-seven years, the father of two daughters, and a twenty-year political veteran. I had worked on numerous campaigns, including three of my own.

One evening my thirty-two-year-old challenger and I engaged in a debate before the Bloomington, Illinois, police union. My opponent referred to my job performance as "garbage." I called him "clueless." On the way out of the building after the debate, I told him he should get his facts straight next time. It was the last nonprofane sentence either of us said. Side-by-side, we walked out the door exchanging epithets of escalating anger, crossing the street to where I had parked my car. I got in on the driver's side. He stepped toward the car door, probably wanting the last word as much as I did. Then he shoved his hand against my shoulder.

I went off like a firecracker. I leapt from my seated position and started swinging. We scuffled with each other back across the street. I missed every punch I threw (though he later disputed this). However, I did manage to kick him squarely in the groin. The fight was over. I noticed there were several people at the end of the block. A police detective was leaving the building where my opponent and I had debated. In an instant, the heat of my anger yielded to a flood of embarrassment.

My opponent claimed I had attacked him. The detective quickly directed all of us, witnesses included, to the police department. My opponent initially indicated that he wanted no further action taken, but after consulting with his advisors, he told the police he wanted charges filed against me. He claimed he never touched me; that he had not come within even six feet of my car; and that I, unprovoked, had attacked him in the middle of the street.

After the police took our statements, I was released and went home. I had to tell my wife that I had been in a street fight, that the police were investigating the matter, and that charges might be filed. It was also necessary to tell my daughters—one by telephone (she was away in college) and the other in person—that their *father* might be accused of a crime. A crime-scene technician came to my home at 2:00 a.m. and examined my car for fingerprints.

The following morning, a story appeared in the local newspaper. I gave an impromptu news conference that day in which I acknowledged the embarrassment of what had occurred and gave my version of the events, which was significantly different from that of my opponent. My picture was taken and appeared in the following morning's paper. It depicted me, quite accurately, as an exhausted and bewildered person, burdened by shame. Because I was an officer of the court in that district, the chief of police requested that a special prosecutor investigate whether felony charges of aggravated battery on a public way should be filed against me or my opponent (though I had not pressed charges against him).

Both of us street warriors took polygraph examinations. The editorial board of the local newspaper called on me to step down from office during the investigation and to resign if I was charged. There was a constant swirl of criticism as well as many expressions of empathy and support. The special prosecutor worked through Thanksgiving and Christmas to resolve the matter. It was not until New Year's Eve that he filed his report to the chief judge. The special prosecutor declined to file charges against either of us. He did, however, note in his public report that I and my opponent, both of us attorneys, had brought disrepute upon ourselves and the legal profession. The community deserved better. However, there is no escaping one simple fact: my participation in this incident was entirely my *responsibility*.

The incident affected not just my public image, but caused me to feel diminished within my family. My wife and daughters, as if they did not already know it, now had living, breathing proof of my imperfections, including, but not limited to, my raging problems of pride and anger. Only over time did I begin to recognize this mistake for what it was: a startling wake-up call. As Merwin says of his mistakes, "you are the ones / I must have needed / the ones who led me / in spite of all that / was said about you / placing my footsteps / on the only way." These were mistakes, perhaps defects in character, that had existed long before this incident and likely "never will leave me / forever after." But I learned a great deal about myself from this incident. I learned that I had to accept these parts of myself before I could meaningfully respond to the challenge of changing them.

After the flurry of publicity began to die down, many friends told me not to worry, to forget about the embarrassment I had experienced. My wife and my daughters said they forgave me. But the traditional connection between forgiving and forgetting, as the old saying goes, suddenly didn't seem so clear to me.

Is it wise to forgive *and* forget? The logic of the aphorism is that by the act of forgiveness, we can forget about the pain we have suffered and not give our grievances opportunity to fester and grow. This logic may prove compelling when we are forgiving others, but I don't think it is very useful when we respond to the burdens of our own mistakes, when we try to forgive ourselves. Forgetting our mistakes diminishes our capacity to correct them. Yet Merwin seems to be saying that our mistakes are *parts* of ourselves, in need of acceptance and integration. His counterintuitive wisdom is that mistakes are our own, they won't simply leave us. They are not to be forgotten or foisted on anyone else. We need them. They lead us.

Merwin's poem is not expressly theological. But for me, it reaches into the heart of divine mercy. Recognition and acceptance of my own mistakes are essential to forgiveness of myself, which is, I believe, the most powerful form of forgiveness. Until I recognize my mistakes I can't really understand my need for forgiveness. And until I experience God's forgiveness I am hardly capable of expressing forgiveness to myself or anyone else. After we have experienced forgiveness, we begin to learn what it feels like to be whole, to have been touched by the divine. Before this experience of brokenness and healing, I did not know that brokenness is more meaningful when shared with others rather than hidden from them.

For me, this is an ongoing work; it is most certainly incomplete. I have made many mistakes before and since the 1996 campaign. I have had the privilege of making numerous mistakes on the front page of the newspaper. These were devastating events, enormously embarrassing to my family and me. However, the more private mistakes have been no less soul shaking, including the ones leading to the dissolution of my marriage and the profound trauma experienced by my daughters. But I now consider my mistakes as alarms, unspeakably difficult, yet necessary steps to becoming more aware and alive.

Several years ago I discovered the Italian word for patience, *pazienza.* It resonated because of my recognition that pride, anger, and *impatience,* the kind I exhibited with my opponent that fateful night, have been constant companions on my journey. They are partners in virtually all my self-destructive enterprises. I examined the word and looked it up in a dictionary I had received during a trip to Italy the year following my campaign. For the first time, I realized the root of this word comes from *pax* or *pacem,* Latin for peace. Within patience, there is peace. So simple, yet so startling. I don't believe I would have gained this insight had I not recognized and finally accepted my own impatience as an integral part of me. I don't always have to give in to this impatience, but I do have to recognize it as part of what makes me tick. As Merwin suggests at the end of his poem, our flaws and mistakes lead us to a deeper understanding of ourselves and life—"placing [our] footsteps / on the only way."

PART FOUR

SIMPLICITY

Twinings Orange Pekoe
Judith Moffett

The gas ring's hoarse exhaling wheeze,
Voice of blue flamelets, licks the kettle's
Copper underbelly, which crouches
Closer, concentrates, by degrees

Begins spellbound to match that pressure
And dragon tone. Breath crowds the slim
Tranced throat that cannot close or scream;
It spouts a rushing *whoo* of pleasure.

The brown potbellied pot, top doffed,
Reveals its scalded insides' tender
Nursery blue, from which a cloud
Exudes, and from its spout a slender

Curl. It sweats and loves the *tch*
A lid makes popping off a tin,
The fragrance deep as leafmold, rich
As pipe tobacco, coffee, cocoa;

Loves the spoon's dry *scroop,* the skin-
Tight leafheap scattered in its breast
(A tannic prickle); the swift boiling
Flashflood, spoonswirl, settling flight; loves best

The steeping in the dark: blind alchemy:
Tap water, and an acid that cures leather
Stains cups and eats through glazes, pregnantly
Stewing together,

To arch forth in a stream as brown and bright
And smoky as an eye, strain marbling up
Through milk and sugar in a stoneware cup,
White white on white.

"A Comfortable Cup of Tea"

JV

IN THE JAPANESE CULTURE, there is a phrase to describe the person who looks out at the world without passion. It is said that person "has no tea in him."

I love the passion in Judith Moffett's poem, cloaked, as it is, in simplicity. Her *Twinings Orange Pekoe* has been like an old friend who disappears for a while from my life, then pops up again, our bond still strong. Each time we meet, I discover new connections to the poem.

I first heard *Twinings Orange Pekoe* read by a Trappist monk at a one-day retreat for busy young professionals struggling to get more in touch with the sacred in the everyday. Work and career dominated my life back then. I was what you might call a "seven-dayer." I thought nothing of going into the office on a Saturday or Sunday. In fact, I felt compelled to. Work was that integral to my life. Father Dennis read several poems at the retreat. Some folks complained about that. What did a poem about making a cup of tea have to do with spirituality! Poetry, especially when you hear a poem read for the first time, forces you to slow down, to listen intently, to live in the moment, or else the poem will pass you right by. I suspect that, for many people at the retreat, this was a problem.

Perhaps because I'm an inveterate tea drinker, I immediately fell in love with the poem. Moffett affectionately and exactingly details this routine act. The poem is a sensual feast from the very first line, when she talks about the "hoarse exhaling wheeze" of the "blue flamelets" flowing out of the stove's gas ring. She imagines the kettle's copper bottom as its hard underbelly. Its spout is a "slim / Tranced throat that cannot close or scream." It exhales a "*whoo* of pleasure" as the water inside heats up by degrees.

Then the eye of the poem turns to the teapot, brown and "potbellied" with scalded insides, the color of nursery blue. It moves to the tin of loose tea, the ticking sound, or more accurately, the "*tch*" sound the lid makes as it pops off, and then the fragrance that greets us, deep as "leafmold, rich / As pipe tobacco, coffee, cocoa." Can't you just taste the tea in your mouth? What the teapot loves best, Moffett imagines, is the "steeping in the dark," the mysterious time when the dark leaves are transubstantiated in this ordinary consecration into a new form: an amber liquid "smoky as an eye." Still today, the English traditionally put the milk in the teacup before the tea. Thus the poem ends with a dark stream marbling up through a pure vision of milk and sugar: "White white on white."

What amazed me about the poem was how Moffett managed to elevate to sacred ritual the simple act of making tea. I imagine her in a cramped, perhaps drafty kitchen on one of those mornings when it's still dark at 6:00 a.m., moving slowly through the making of tea. Perhaps she spends this time contemplating the day ahead or meditating on what is unfolding in her life. I imagine the sound of wind chimes coming from a porch. The point Father Dennis tried to make is that our lives are filled with all sorts of small rituals we may not even be conscious of. It might be something as routine as finishing the crossword puzzle every night before bed, eating out on Friday nights, or the way we fold our socks. Or it could be as conscious as where we spend Thanksgiving, the pew we choose at church, the route we follow to work. Because we do these acts repeatedly, they are important to us. When we consider their value, they also become sacred. It occurs to me how ingenious Jesus was to choose as his memorial the ordinary staples of the Middle Eastern dinner table: bread and wine. How perceptive the early church leaders were to refer to this ritual, not as a eulogy, but a eucharist, a thanksgiving. If Christ had appeared in the Orient and not the Middle East, we likely would be consecrating not wine but tea at communion!

Moffett's *Twinings Orange Pekoe* remained dormant in my mind for several years. Then, like a trusted friend, it reemerged when I moved to London in 1994 to work as a foreign correspondent for the *Wall Street Journal*. London was and is serious tea country. When I moved there, I brought with me the ceramic teapot I had purchased on a vacation a few years before in New Zealand. I took to buying only loose tea, preferably Twinings. My London tour was one of the loneliest periods of my life. I was single and unattached then. All the other reporters I worked with were married or in relationships. Although I've always had a friendly, outgoing personality, I found it difficult to crack the British reserve and make friends. You had to be introduced, almost vouched for, in order for a Londoner to "take you on" as a friend.

Sometimes kindness came from the most unexpected people, and was so much the more welcome. Almost always, these moments surrounded a cup of tea. One such incident occurred soon after I had arrived in London to look for a place to live. I was staying at the home of some colleagues in Hampstead, on London's northwest side, while they were visiting the U.S. One evening when I returned home, I could not get the key to unlock the front door. I asked some neighbors for help, and when they couldn't unlock the door, they suggested I call a locksmith. A strapping Irishman who looked to be ageless arrived. With a few deft movements of his slender tools, he swiftly sorted out the problem. I invited him to stay for a cup of tea. He seemed rather taken aback at first. Eventually he told me that the class system was still very much in evidence. The English rarely if ever extended such an invitation to hired help. (It's possible things have changed since then.) He asked what I was doing in London, and I spoke of my anxieties about starting a new job, my worries about making friends in a new country. As an expatriate too, he empathized with me.

I put on the kettle and was poised to scoop some tea leaves into a teapot when I noticed the locksmith watching me intently. Finally he said, "Would you like to learn how to make a proper cup of tea?" He proceeded to inform me. You heat the water in your kettle. Then, into the empty teapot, you swirl a small amount of the boiling water, to warm it up. Pour that water out, and fill the pot with a new dose of boiling water. Add the tea leaves slowly, stirring them occasionally. Drop in a tiny bit of cold water to "settle the leaves." While the tea brews, pour milk into the teacup, sugar, too, if desired. Lastly, the most important step in the process: wait.

The step-by-step movements and the waiting turned this ordinary act into an event. I have no idea if what my locksmith friend described is truly the proper way to make tea. But I do know I was happiest in London whenever I could invite someone over to my flat and perform the ritual which Moffett called, "The steeping in the dark: blind alchemy."

Not long ago, I pulled from my bookcase a title I hadn't looked at for years. It is Okakura Kakuzo's classic, *The Book of Tea*. Kakuzo calls tea "the cup of humanity."

> When we consider how small after all the cup of human enjoyment is, how soon overflowed with tears, how easily drained to the dregs in our quenchless thirst for infinity, we shall not blame ourselves for making so much of the teacup.

Throughout history, Buddhist monks would gather before an image of their spiritual leader. They drank tea out of a single bowl during their meditation as a way of being in communion with each other and the almighty. This practice evolved into the tea ceremony, which many Japanese—and a growing number of Americans—practice in their homes. The ceremony combines tea making, art, architecture, and poetry to create for one's guests an atmosphere of hospitality, harmony, and peace. For the Japanese and Chinese, even the type of teapots, teacups, and utensils one uses carries significance.

I was delighted when I read that the ancient Chinese considered blue the ideal color for the inside of a teapot or teacup; it is the same color as the inside of Moffett's pot.

When I was working on this book, Judith Moffett, now living in Lawrenceburg, Kentucky, was kind enough to answer a few questions about the poem. She wrote the poem in, of all places, Stockholm during the winter of 1976–77. She was there on a writing fellowship from the Ingram-Merrill Foundation. She had started drinking tea for the first time in her life on an earlier stay in Sweden, as a Fulbright scholar. As she describes it:

> I was twenty-five and had never liked coffee *or* tea. But when our group of Fulbrighters arrived to be oriented, we were given intensive lessons in Swedish using a new ear-only approach (idiotic to try that on a bunch of academics!). This was exhausting, and the little coffee, tea, and pastry interludes in our days were so vital that I had to try *something*. So I went with tea, the least formidable of the options.

Moffett borrowed from some Swedish friends a small brown teapot with a blue lining made of Denby stoneware. When she went on to study in England, she found and bought a pot exactly like it and took that one back home with her to the U.S. She recalled,

> Since my first long stay in England in the fall of 1970, afternoon tea has been making its welcome daily

punctuation mark in my long working days. I get to
have some sort of little pastry thing with it, and I get
to read fiction or something for pleasure. My tea tray
stands ready on the counter: pot, cup, saucer, spoon,
sugar bowl, small plate, milk jug, arranged in a certain
pattern that hasn't changed in decades.

Moffett revealed that in the poem she was preparing her
breakfast tray, not her afternoon tea tray. At the time, she says,
she couldn't have imagined how that ritual would "continue as
a vital tradition through many relocations and life situations."
When Moffett met the man who was to become her husband,
an early bond between them was their mutual fondness for
afternoon tea. But at the time Moffett wrote this poem, she did
not yet know her husband. "All that was in the future," she told
me, "But I do feel it's somehow implicit in the poem."

I had a similar experience of my future being glimpsed
in my past when I first met my fiancé Charles Reynard's old-
est daughter, Rachel. Charley had been divorced for two years
when we met. Still, it must have been painful for Rachel to
see her father in a serious relationship with a woman who
was not her mother. During our first meeting, I learned that
Rachel and I are both serious tea drinkers. I told Rachel my
story of the locksmith who taught me how to make a "proper
cup of tea." We both had a good laugh. A few months later,
on my birthday, Rachel and her husband surprised me with
a box of Scottish shortbreads and two lovely canisters of spe-
cialty tea—Honey Ginseng Green and Botswana Blossom
Red. (The shortbreads, I supposed, were a paean to my Celtic

handyman). I knew then that Rachel and I had connected. Tea would always be a bond.

The making and sharing of tea is just one of the simple rituals I've come to love. There are many others in my life: weekday Mass mornings at 8:15, then a cup of vanilla cappuccino and playing scratch-offs in the Illinois lottery with my retired friends Tillie, Ellen, Helen, Don, and Donny; watching the baseball play-offs and the World Series every year; traveling to Starved Rock State Park to see the changing leaves each fall; listening to National Public Radio in the morning. All of these rituals weave together in my life. They remind me that living is a work of art, one we quilt together for ourselves through thousands of small moments.

Not long ago, I attended a Founders' Day service at St. Xavier University in Chicago, which is run by the Sisters of Mercy. One of the sisters on staff related the courageous exploits of their order's founder, Catherine McAuley. The sisters like to tell a story about Mother McAuley's last words. As she lay dying, her followers racked in agonizing grief, she sent a final message to her devoted sisters. At the moment she passed, they were to fortify themselves with a "comfortable cup of tea."

Judith Moffett, like Catherine McAuley and Kakuzo before her, recognized that we draw strength from the simplest, most common rituals. May we always, as Kakuzo urges in *The Book of Tea*, find ways to rejoice in "the beautiful foolishness of things."

AIMLESS LOVE
Billy Collins

This morning as I walked along the lakeshore,
I fell in love with a wren
and later in the day with a mouse
the cat had dropped under the dining room table.

In the shadows of an autumn evening,
I fell for a seamstress
still at her machine in the tailor's window,
and later for a bowl of broth,
steam rising like smoke from a naval battle.

This is the best kind of love, I thought,
without recompense, without gifts,
or unkind words, without suspicion,
or silence on the telephone.

The love of the chestnut,
the jazz cap and one hand on the wheel.

No lust, no slam of the door—
the love of the miniature orange tree,
the clean white shirt, the hot evening shower,
the highway that cuts across Florida.

No waiting, no huffiness, or rancor—
just a twinge every now and then

for the wren who had built her nest
on a low branch overhanging the water
and for the dead mouse,
still dressed in its light brown suit.

But my heart is always propped up
in a field on its tripod,
ready for the next arrow.

After I carried the mouse by the tail
to a pile of leaves in the woods,
I found myself standing at the bathroom sink
gazing down affectionately at the soap,

so patient and soluble,
so at home in its pale green soap dish.
I could feel myself falling again
as I felt its turning in my wet hands
and caught the scent of lavender and stone.

The Art of Complication
CR

I HAVE DEVOTED A GOOD portion of my life to the art of complication. My chosen profession is the law. I confess to an almost obsessive fascination with the intricacies and serpentine qualities of our legal system. As a Circuit Court judge, I preside over everything from data-packed personal injury cases to emotionally charged family disputes. On a daily basis, I must sort through a tangle of fact, perception, and, yes, fiction. The public expects—no, *demands*—that I find within that thicket an answer that bears some semblance to justice and pays at least minimal homage to the truth. As a trial attorney, I may have sought to obfuscate. As a judge, I'm expected to clarify.

This is perhaps why I am so drawn to the poems of former U.S. poet laureate Billy Collins, and this poem in particular: it is because of his appreciation of the art of simplicity. Here is a man who can fall in love with a miniature orange tree, his crisply laundered white shirt, or the sight of a "dead mouse, / still dressed in its light brown suit." This is a man as "patient and soluble" as the bar of soap he finds himself gazing at on his bathroom sink. The kind of man I'd like to be and wish I had been.

Loving County in west Texas is one of the least populated counties in America. Loving's claim to fame is that not one of its residents holds a law degree. In surrounding counties, locals say, rattlesnakes outnumber attorneys. Loving's chief deputy sheriff once commented, "Goodness, if you've got to have rattlesnakes or lawyers, which one would you have?" That was not how I viewed it growing up in 1950s America. I absorbed myself in TV legal dramas. Perry Mason, Paul Drake, Della Street: I loved them and their tireless efforts to untangle the secrets that *always* caused their clients to be accused unjustly. I was devoted to *The Defenders,* its father-and-son team of E. G. Marshall and Robert Reed, who advocated for justice against great odds. John F. Kennedy, Robert Kennedy, and Martin Luther King Jr. were my heroes. By the time I was fifteen, my fully formed ambition was to become a courtroom advocate in the style of my television heroes and to advance the social causes of my three political heroes.

In the fall of 1968, the year of the King and Robert Kennedy assassinations, I was admitted to the evening division of Loyola University Law School. I attended law school at night and kept my job teaching language arts at DeVry Technical Institute during the day. How in the world my fiancée and I thought we could get married following my first semester in law school, while she was still a junior in college, remains a testimony to our immaturity and inflated sense of our own ability for multitasking! In less than two years, she and I separated. I dropped out of law school for eighteen months while we sought to piece together our marriage through counseling.

We reunited after eight months, and then separated again for two months. The fact that I was nearing the end of law school gave us both hope, and we reunited yet again. It was a proper but not perfectly placed hope. In my first year of private practice, I worked for Legal Aid in Chicago. Then I heard about a position as an assistant state's attorney in McLean County in central Illinois. We packed up our fragile marriage and moved there in 1970. I worked hard at being a good prosecutor. Unfortunately, this meant that I was not fully attentive to my marriage. The law remained the proverbial "jealous mistress." My wife often felt neglected, excluded from the bulk of my life. Notwithstanding these unresolved issues, our first daughter was born in 1977.

Motivated by a desire to give my growing family greater financial security and a better quality of life, I resigned from government and entered private practice. Working as a solo practitioner and later as senior partner in a two-lawyer office were both considerably more demanding than I had expected. To further complicate matters, I became involved in local politics (undoubtedly to patronize those heroic ambitions of my youth). Against my wife's wishes (though she ultimately assented), I ran for state's attorney in 1980 and lost. I remained active in the community, however, and continued to negotiate with my wife over the demands of my law practice and burgeoning public career. These negotiations were never fully successful. My inability to arrive at a satisfactory balance remained a major strain in our marriage, but we remained together. Our second daughter arrived in late 1982, and we worked hard as a team to raise our daughters.

Five years later, I received the professional break I had long desired. I was appointed state's attorney to fill a midterm vacancy left by the incumbent. I threw myself into that job for the next sixteen years. I made the prevention of domestic violence a cornerstone of my administration. I vigorously prosecuted child abuse, sexual assault, and nonpayment of child support. My own domestic life, meanwhile, remained a roller-coaster ride of escalating challenges. If one had accused me in a court of law of being an insufficiently attentive husband and self-centered man, I suspect the judge would have ruled, "guilty as charged." The truth is, my marriage might have limped on, but the chaotic life of lawyering, combined with my public service, depleted the vital supply of nutrients a marriage needs to survive. My wife and I were simply emotionally dehydrated. In 2000, we separated for the last time. Our divorce became final in 2002.

One night, as I lay in bed reading Collins's *Aimless Love,* I thought of my failed marriage. Oh to have been the kind of man who could revel in what simply is, who could seek what Collins calls "the best kind of love":

> without recompense, without gifts,
> or unkind words, without suspicion,
> or silence on the telephone.
>
> The love of the chestnut,
> the jazz cap and one hand on the wheel.

The next morning, in a break from the considerable volume of civil cases, I chatted informally with one of the defense attorneys. He shared that he was about to leave on a two-week vacation to explore the Grand Canyon with his wife and children. I applauded his efforts to spend time with his family doing something so memorable. Then he described how his vacations went. He would wake up before the rest of the family to make phone calls and work a few hours on legal briefs. He and his wife had agreed beforehand on this compartmentalization of his time.

Then he told me the story of his wedding day. That morning, he went to his office to tie up a few loose ends. He became absorbed in a pretrial motion. At one point he glanced at his watch and realized he would be late for his wedding. Despite breaking a series of speed limits, he arrived at the church in time for the ceremony, but not the prewedding photos. Somehow, his bride understood and forgave all, even when he stopped by the office for several more hours before they left on their honeymoon! I commended the young attorney for having such a saintly spouse.

Couples today experience even more demands on their time than my former wife and I did thirty years ago. She was able to be at home for most of my daughters' early years. Today, most couples are by necessity two-earner families. An increasing array of professional, educational, and recreational opportunities can enrich a couple's life, but striking a balance becomes more difficult. As a culture we seem afflicted by a form of attention deficit/hyperactivity disorder. We are profoundly driven to distraction.

Not surprisingly, an entire industry in the form of books, workshops, newsletters, and Web sites has grown up around our collective hunger for greater simplicity. One site offers literally hundreds of bromides and quotes from the ancient Greeks to Albert Einstein on the virtues of simplicity:

- "Beauty of style and harmony and grace and good rhythm depend on simplicity" (Plato).

- "The firm, the enduring, the simple, and the modest are near to virtue" (Confucius).

- "We act as though comfort and luxury were the chief requirements of life, when all that we need to make us happy is something to be enthusiastic about" (Charles Kingsley).

- "It is no use walking anywhere to preach unless our walking is our preaching" (St. Francis of Assisi).

- "When the solution is simple, God is answering" (Albert Einstein).

I particularly like this observation from the thirteenth-century Persian poet Rumi: "Only let the moving waters calm down, and the sun and moon will be reflected in the surface of your being."

The difficulty, of course, is taking these prescriptions and applying them to the real life of every day. That is less simple. In fact, simplifying our life is so complex that many of us feel compelled to sign up for a workshop to break it down into simple steps. Which is why I happen to like Billy Collins's prescription best of all. He merely asks us to look for those luminous moments that shine through any day. Those moments when we walk along a lakeshore and fall in love with a wren, when we sit in awe before a steaming bowl of broth or enjoy the sensate experience of washing our hands with a bar of lavender-scented soap. For that, it is necessary merely to keep our hearts propped up as if on a tripod, "ready for the next arrow." The best love is aimless. The best love simply is.

PART FIVE

PRAISE

THE GREATEST GRANDEUR
Pattiann Rogers

Some say it's in the reptilian dance
of the purple-tongued sand goanna,
for there the magnificent translation
of tenacity into bone and grace occurs.

And some declare it to be an expansive
desert—solid rust-orange rock
like dusk captured on earth in stone—
simply for the perfect contrast it provides
to the blue-grey ridge of rain
in the distant hills.

Some claim the harmonics of shifting
electron rings to be most rare and some
the complex motion of seven sandpipers
bisecting the arcs and pitches
of come and retreat over the mounting
hayfield.

Others, for grandeur, choose the terror
of lightning peals on prairies or the tall
collapsing cathedrals of stormy seas,
because there they feel dwarfed
and appropriately helpless; others select
the serenity of that ceiling/cellar
of stars they see at night on placid lakes,

because there they feel assured
and universally magnanimous.

But it is the dark emptiness contained
in every next moment that seems to me
the most singularly glorious gift,
that void which one is free to fill
with processions of men bearing burning
cedar knots or with parades of blue horses,
belled and ribboned and stepping sideways,
with tumbling white-faced mimes or companies
of black-robed choristers; to fill simply
with hammered silver teapots or kiln-dried
crockery, tangerine and almond custards,
polonaises, polkas, whittling sticks, wailing
walls; that space large enough to hold all
invented blasphemies and pieties, 10,000
definitions of god and more, never fully
filled, never.

TEN THOUSAND DEFINITIONS OF GOD
IV

THE POET LISEL MUELLER once joked that Pattiann Rogers was determined to mention every specimen of flora and fauna in her poems. Rogers's fluency in science makes her poems somewhat jarring at first. We are as likely to find there lascivious oak toads and African dung beetle eggs as we are electrons and cells, salt domes and savannahs. Under Rogers's skilled pen, near microscopic observations of the natural world turn into grand celebrations of life.

I met Pattiann Rogers once in 1998, when she gave a reading for the Poetry Center of Chicago. She is a witty, self-effacing woman, who still speaks with a thick Southern drawl. The reading took place at the dinner hour. At one point, she stopped between poems to inquire of the audience, "Are y'all getting hungry?"

Rogers's poems teach me things I didn't know about before, say, the sex lives of hummingbirds, the eccentricities of tomcats. It is as if in each poem, Rogers is saying, "How can there possibly be this much to marvel at?" Often, she sees the world from a peculiar perspective, as in the poem *The Answering of Prayers,* where she contemplates the iris:

Because they have neither tongue
Nor voice, the iris are thought by some
Never to pray, also because they have no hands

Of all the poems she read at the Poetry Center, none struck me more than *The Greatest Grandeur.* She chose this poem to read at her son's wedding. "It's after all a poem about the future and possibility. Very apt for a wedding," she told me later. Rogers's poem shares much in common with Gerard Manley Hopkins's famous work *God's Grandeur:*

The world is charged with the grandeur of God.
    It will flame out, like shining from shook foil;
    It gathers to a greatness, like the ooze of oil
Crushed. Why do men then now not reck his rod?
Generations have trod, have trod, have trod;
    And all is seared with trade; bleared, smeared with toil;
    And wears man's smudge and shares man's smell: the soil
Is bare now, nor can foot feel, being shod.

And for all this, nature is never spent;
    There lives the dearest freshness deep down things;
And though the last lights off the black West went,
    Oh, morning, at the brown brink eastward, springs—
Because the Holy Ghost over the bent
    World broods with warm breast and with ah! bright wings.

The poems of both Hopkins and Rogers provide a litany of grandeur. For Hopkins, grandeur flames out like "shook foil" (tinsel). Hopkins, who lived at the start of the Industrial Age, believed awe could be experienced in an industrialized city as well as in a bucolic setting. I suspect that most people who've stood at street level staring up at the soaring steel outline of the Sears Tower in Chicago have felt that awe. Grandeur also gathers like oil, the poet says—an allusion by the Jesuit Hopkins, no doubt, to the oil used to anoint the sick and dying or a newly ordained priest's hands. Hopkins might also mean ordinary cooking oil: God's grandeur found in the home, in the stuff of everyday living.

In Hopkins's view, the world is ever renewing, "never spent." It is man who destroys, who trods and trods. Earth "wears man's smudge," shares his smell. But morning somehow always manages to arrive. According to Hopkins, the spirit of God never stops embracing the world, turning the dark nights of our souls into the dawns of resurrection.

Hopkins believed that a sacredness lies at the core of all things, what he called "the dearest freshness deep down things." He coined a word for this. He called it "inscape." Hopkins believed if we remain attuned to the world around us, we will eventually discover this distinctiveness, this sacredness at the core of everything. For Hopkins, it is a sacredness that arises from Christ's entry into the world, from Christ's incarnation, his literally becoming flesh. Hopkins probably drew this notion, too, from his understanding of the Catholic sacraments, in which outward acts become sources of inward grace. His Jesuit training had taught him the imperative of his order's founder, St. Ignatius of Loyola, to find God in all things.

Rogers also draws her evidence from the everyday world. Her litany of God's grandeur is just as wild and diverse as Hopkins's. She finds it in the oddest creatures, like "the purple-tongued sand goanna," for who could have imagined such a being, its peculiar reptilian grace? She finds it in a vast expanse of desert. Think of the land outside Tucson, say, where rock and earth appear to have absorbed the burnt-orange colors of dusk. She sees it also in the atoms that form all matter; in the balletic movements of seven sandpipers slicing the air; in lightning, stars, and tall waves, which Rogers beautifully describes as "collapsing cathedrals of stormy seas."

Rogers once recounted to me how her poem came to be. "The poem began with my asking myself the question: what is the greatest gift we are given? I didn't know the answer to that question, but I wanted to write a poem exploring it. . . . I started composing a list of what I regarded as wonderful gifts, features of the earth and various life forms and experiences important to me."

I have always loved the last stanza of Rogers's poem best. There she suggests that of all the universe's singular gifts, the greatest grandeur lies in "every next moment," in the what is to come. It's interesting that Rogers doesn't say in "every next moment of joy" but quite simply *every* moment. Something of mystery and sacredness lies even in those desert seasons of our lives, when we experience sickness, sadness, or despair. Rogers told me that when she was writing the poem, "Everything I listed I considered not just a great but a grand and treasured gift. Yet none seemed grander to me than any other. Then, after working through many drafts of the poem, the thought expressed in the final stanza of the poem came to me, something that I had never thought of before. Something so common and ever-present that I never really considered it a gift before, and yet it seemed obviously to be 'the greatest grandeur.'"

Toward the end of his life, Hopkins wrote a series of poems known as the "terrible sonnets." He believed he had failed to reach his full potential as poet and priest. He referred to himself as "time's eunuch." He wrote,

Birds build—but not I build; no but strain,
Time's eunuch, and not breed one work that wakes.

Still, Hopkins found strength within himself to praise these painful seasons and find meaning in his challenges. In a commentary on the *Spiritual Exercises* of St. Ignatius, he wrote, "Any day, any minute we bless God for our being or for anything, for food, for sunlight, we do and are what we were meant for, made for—things that give and mean to give God glory. This is a thing to live for."

I think that's what Rogers is driving at when she speaks of "every next moment." I am reminded of the final line in Stephen Sondheim's musical *Sunday in the Park with George,* where the artist contemplates perhaps the greatest color of all: "White, the color of a blank page or canvas. So many possibilities." Rogers seems to be saying that time is arguably our most precious possession. Time, a blank page pregnant with possibilities, which we are free to fill as we choose, she says, with parades of belled and ribboned horses, with tangerine custard and kiln-dried crockery, with polonaises and polkas, teapots and whittling sticks, and much, much more. Each moment of life is spacious enough to accommodate "10,000 / definitions of god." The ways we experience God in the world can never be exhausted. Both Rogers and Hopkins would agree that there exists a sacredness so vast that it goes on forever, "never fully / filled, never." We stand in awe and offer our praise.

Excerpts from Song of Myself
Walt Whitman

1

I celebrate myself, and sing myself,
And what I assume you shall assume,
For every atom belonging to me as good belongs to you.

I loafe and invite my soul,
I lean and loafe at my ease observing a spear of summer
　　grass.

My tongue, every atom of my blood, form'd from this soil,
　　this air,
Born here of parents born here from parents the same, and
　　their parents the same,
I, now thirty-seven years old in perfect health begin,
Hoping to cease not till death.

2

. . . .

Have you reckon'd a thousand acres much? Have you
　　reckon'd the earth much?
Have you practis'd so long to learn to read?
Have you felt so proud to get at the meaning of poems?

Stop this day and night with me and you shall possess the
　　origin of all poems,

You shall possess the good of the earth and sun, (there are
    millions of suns left,)
You shall no longer take things at second or third hand, nor
    look through the eyes of the dead, nor feed on the spectres
    in books,
You shall not look through my eyes either, nor take things
    from me,
You shall listen to all sides and filter them from your self.

3

I have heard what the talkers were talking, the talk of the
    beginning and the end,
But I do not talk of the beginning or the end.
There was never any more inception than there is now,
Nor any more youth or age than there is now,
And will never be any more perfection than there is now,
Nor any more heaven or hell than there is now.
. . . .
I and this mystery here we stand.
. . . .

5

. . . .
Swiftly arose and spread around me the peace and
    knowledge that pass all the argument of the earth,
And I know that the hand of God is the promise of my own,
And I know that the spirit of God is the brother of my own,
And that all the men ever born are also my brothers, and the
    women my sisters and lovers,

And that a kelson of the creation is love,
And limitless are leaves stiff or drooping in the fields,
And brown ants in the little wells beneath them,
And mossy scabs of the worm fence, heap'd stones, elder,
    mullein and poke-weed.

6

A child said *What is the grass?* fetching it to me with full
    hands;
How could I answer the child? I do not know what it is any
    more than he.

I guess it must be the flag of my disposition, out of hopeful
    green stuff woven.

Or I guess it is the handkerchief of the Lord,
A scented gift and remembrancer designedly dropt,
Bearing the owner's name someway in the corners, that we
    may see and remark, and say *Whose?*

Or I guess the grass is itself a child, the produced babe of the
    vegetation.

Or I guess it is a uniform hieroglyphic,
And it means, Sprouting alike in broad zones and narrow
    zones,
Growing among black folks as among white,
Kanuck, Tuckahoe, Congressman, Cuff, I give them the
    same, I receive them the same.

And now it seems to me the beautiful uncut hair of graves.

. . . .

What do you think has become of the young and old men?
And what do you think has become of the women and
    children?

They are alive and well somewhere,
The smallest sprout shows there is really no death,
And if ever there was it led forward life, and does not wait at
    the end to arrest it,
And ceas'd the moment life appear'd.

All goes onward and outward, nothing collapses,
And to die is different from what any one supposed, and
    luckier.

7

. . . .

I pass death with the dying and birth with the new-wash'd
    babe and am not contained between my hat and my boots,
And peruse manifold objects, not two alike and every one
    good,
The earth good and the stars good, and their adjuncts all
    good.

. . . .

20

. . . .

I know I am deathless,

I know this orbit of mine cannot be swept by a carpenter's
compass,

I know I shall not pass like a child's carlacue cut with a burnt
stick at night.

I know I am august,

I do not trouble my spirit to vindicate itself or be
understood,

I see that the elementary laws never apologize,

(I reckon I behave no prouder than the level I plant my house
by, after all.)

I exist as I am, that is enough,

If no other in the world be aware I sit content,

And if each and all be aware I sit content.

One world is aware and by far the largest to me, and that is
myself,

And whether I come to my own to-day or in ten thousand or
ten million years,

I can cheerfully take it now, or with equal cheerfulness I can
wait.

My foothold is tenon'd and mortis'd in granite,
I laugh at what you call dissolution,
And I know the amplitude of time.

21

I am the poet of the Body and I am the poet of the Soul,
The pleasures of heaven are with me and the pains of hell are
    with me,
The first I graft and increase upon myself, the latter I
    translate into a new tongue.

I am the poet of the woman the same as the man,
And I say it is as great to be a woman as to be a man,
And I say there is nothing greater than the mother of men.

. . . .

24

. . . .

I believe in the flesh and the appetites,
Seeing, hearing, feeling, are miracles, and each part and tag
    of me is a miracle.

Divine am I inside and out, and I make holy whatever I
    touch or am touch'd from,
The scent of these arm-pits aroma finer than prayer,
This head more than churches, bibles, and all the creeds.

. . . .

48

. . . .

I hear and behold God in every object, yet understand God
not in the least,

Nor do I understand who there can be more wonderful than
myself.

Why should I wish to see God better than this day?

I see something of God each hour of the twenty-four, and
each moment then,

In the faces of men and women I see God, and in my own
face in the glass,

I find letters from God dropt in the street, and every one is
sign'd by God's name,

And I leave them where they are, for I know that wheresoe'er
I go,

Others will punctually come for ever and ever.

49

And as to you Death, and you bitter hug of mortality, it is
idle to try to alarm me.

. . . .

51

. . . .

Listener up there! what have you to confide to me?

Look in my face while I snuff the sidle of evening,

(Talk honestly, no one else hears you, and I stay only a
    minute longer.)

Do I contradict myself?
Very well then I contradict myself,
(I am large, I contain multitudes.)

. . . .

52

. . . .

I depart as air, I shake my white locks at the runaway sun,
I effuse my flesh in eddies, and drift it in lacy jags.

I bequeath myself to the dirt to grow from the grass I love,
If you want me again look for me under your boot-soles.

You will hardly know who I am or what I mean,
But I shall be good health to you nevertheless,
And filter and fibre your blood.

Failing to fetch me at first keep encouraged,
Missing me one place search another,
I stop somewhere waiting for you.

"How Can I Keep from Singing?"

CR

Song of *Myself* reminds me of a hymn we sang for years at the St. Robert Bellarmine Newman Center in Normal, Illinois. It continues to be a favorite of the small faith group I meet with. The song joyfully recognizes a sense of church in the world as well as the Good News our faith has empowered us to live and to give to ourselves and others:

> My life flows in endless song above earth's lamentation,
> I hear the real though far off hymn that sounds a new
>   creation.
> No storm can shake my inmost calm while to that rock
>   I'm clinging,
> It sounds an echo in my soul. How can I keep from
>   singing?

We live in an antipraise culture. Consider the shock jocks on talk radio and the shouting matches that pass for political discourse on cable news shows. Look at our most recent national elections, a process in which questions about character became a means of character assassination. Much of contemporary poetry, too, carries with it a weary cynicism. Walt Whitman stands in sharp contrast. Whitman lived at a time of poverty and upheaval in America's urban centers. He witnessed the suffering of the Civil War. Yet, while he remained a realist, he managed to sidestep cynicism.

Whitman's poem is a hymn of praise to the world. Whitman called it his paean to America. It is a deeply reverent and prayerful work. In the profoundly ordinary, the poem finds the sacred substance of what makes us human. Even so, I would not have thought to include this long, rambling work in the anthology had it not been for a recent visit with my younger daughter, Meghan.

She and her older sister, Rachel, have inspired me on many occasions. This inspiration came, like many of the others, amid the most mundane of circumstances. It was Saturday evening, and I was in Meg's Claflin Hall dormitory room at Wellesley College. We had chosen to kick back with a movie and one or two of the microbrews she had received from friends on her twenty-second birthday. We watched *With Honors,* a cute 1994 comedy. Joe Pesci plays a homeless man named Simon Wilder who frequents Harvard University's campus. He becomes the nemesis of Montgomery (Monty) Kessler, played by Brendan Fraser. Simon finds Monty's senior thesis, consisting of over a hundred pages, then holds it for ransom.

Simon nicknames Monty "Harvard" for his elitist approach to education. He offers to return Monty's thesis, page by page, in exchange for a bit of shelter, some meals, and miscellaneous acts of kindness. "Harvard" is annoyed by the presumption of Simon's demands, but grudgingly furnishes Simon with shelter in a broken-down Volkswagen bus. For that, Simon returns several pages of the thesis. To deal with the winter cold, Simon asks for extra blankets in exchange for several more pages. They make similar trades for meals and for a bubble bath.

Simon, we subsequently learn, is dying of asbestosis from exposure to the chemical during his years of building ships for the merchant marines. In spite of his desperate health circumstances, perhaps partially because of them, he conveys to "Harvard" several lessons of redemptive significance. Through his negotiations for the basic necessities of life, Monty begins to see Simon not merely as a bum, but a human being entitled to more consideration and dignity than he has been given. Monty starts out believing that his thesis is his raison d'etre, his ticket to a successful career and happiness in life. He comes to assign more priority to Simon's needs than the deadline for turning in the completed manuscript. Monty chooses to honor Simon's request to see the son he had abandoned years before one time before he dies. As a result of performing this act of mercy, Monty is unable to turn his thesis in on time, thus forfeiting his opportunity to graduate "with honors." Simon, in tearful gratitude, pronounces Monty a graduate "in life, with honors."

Walt Whitman's poetry provides a kind of Greek chorus to the plot. At one point in the story, Simon disappears back into the underworld of the Boston homeless. In one particularly moving scene, another homeless man comes to Monty's door saying that Simon has sent him for a hot meal. Monty gives the homeless man a bowl of soup and a sandwich. The man reads a message from Simon to Monty, written in pencil on the back of yet another of the returned pages:

You shall no longer take things at second or third hand,
  nor look through the eyes of the dead, nor feed on the
  spectres in books,
You shall not look through my eyes either, nor take
  things from me,
You shall listen to all sides and filter them from your self.

The words are from the second section of *Song of Myself.*
At that moment, Monty begins to recognize the challenge he
is really facing. It is the challenge of growing up, of waking up
to his own responsibilities.

In the most poignant scene of all, Simon lays in bed
within minutes of dying. Monty and his other roommates
take turns reading from Simon's constant companion, a
weathered volume of Walt Whitman's *Leaves of Grass.* They
read these excerpts from *Song of Myself.* There were never,
in my opinion, more powerful prayers for the dying than
these:

I am of old and young, of the foolish as much as the wise
. . . .
I depart as air, I shake my white locks at the runaway
  sun,
I effuse my flesh in eddies, and drift it in lacy jags.

I bequeath myself to the dirt to grow from the grass I
  love,
If you want me again look for me under your boot-soles.

You will hardly know who I am or what I mean,
But I shall be good health to you nevertheless,
And filter and fibre your blood.

Failing to fetch me at first keep encouraged,
Missing me one place search another,
I stop somewhere waiting for you.

Meg and I looked at each other as the scene ended. We were both crying. We laughed and then cried some more as the credits rolled. Let the film critics pan this movie all they want. Without question, it is not enduring film literature. But it is a genuinely sweet and endearing movie. Meg and I recalled having watched the film during her Catholic confirmation class six years before. I was one of the teachers, and we had selected it because it carries with it a message of commitment to the welfare of others, particularly for the "least of these my brethren" (Matthew 25:40). The literary critics can also sharply critique Walt Whitman's sweeping sentimentality, as in fact they did during his lifetime. Yet the fact is that poetry interacts with life in its everyday moments, and death is among the most commonplace of those moments. When poetry works its chemistry with life, it brings tears. They are tears of cleansing, clarifying joy. They are redemptive moments of beauty.

In the fifteenth part of *Song of Myself,* not excerpted here due to its extraordinary length, Whitman concocts a seemingly endless catalogue of praise. He praises the contralto, the carpenter, the "married and unmarried children," the pilot, the mate, and the "duck-shooter." Likewise, he singles out "the opium-eater," the prostitute, the President and Secretaries, more than seventy-five kinds of people. He continues on for several more pages. He adds, finally, "And of these one and all I weave the song of myself."

Whitman exhausts us with praise. He celebrates the unity of America. And yet his celebration transcends any notion of politics or national identity. He exalts the oneness of endless diversity. Perhaps he is reaching for a conceptual grasp of God, similar to the Catholic notion of the "mystical body of Christ" in which we are all one.

> I hear and behold God in every object, yet understand
>   God not in the least,
> Nor do I understand who there can be more wonderful
>   than myself.
> Why should I wish to see God better than this day?
> I see something of God each hour of the twenty-four,
>   and each moment then,
> In the faces of men and women I see God, and in my
>   own face in the glass,
> I find letters from God dropt in the street, and every one
>   is sign'd by God's name,
> And I leave them where they are, for I know that
>   wheresoe'er I go,
> Others will punctually come for ever and ever.

Whitman published the first untitled version of these poems in 1855. He continued to edit them and add new poems throughout his career. The version of *Song of Myself* excerpted here was published in the third edition of *Leaves of Grass* in 1883. His joy has not dimmed in the more than one hundred fifty years since their first publication. The openness and unbridled hopefulness of his poetry remain unique in American poetry, even if some in the poetry establishment still view it with a kind of intellectual jaundice.

In reading *Song of Myself,* I, too, become a "singer." There are times I may be distracted, worn down. I may forget that the ordinary moments of my life are the connective tissue joining me with all of creation. To praise may seem counterintuitive in our modern culture. In poetry, it can appear sentimental. Yet it is a necessity with vastly more priority than much of what I take to be important. No matter how inconstant my key or how broken my voice, Whitman's insistent message of praise carries me forward. "How can I keep from singing?"

PART SIX

WORK

AS KINGFISHERS CATCH FIRE, DRAGONFLIES DRAW FLAME

Gerard Manley Hopkins

As kingfishers catch fire, dragonflies draw flame;
As tumbled over rim in roundy wells
Stones ring; like each tucked string tells, each hung bell's
Bow swung finds tongue to fling out broad its name;
Each mortal thing does one thing and the same:
Deals out that being indoors each one dwells;
Selves—goes itself; *myself* it speaks and spells,
Crying *What I do is me: for that I came.*

I say more: the just man justices;
Keeps grace: that keeps all his goings graces;
Acts in God's eye what in God's eye he is—
Christ—for Christ plays in ten thousand places,
Lovely in limbs, and lovely in eyes not his
    To the Father through the feature of men's faces.

For That I Came

IV

At first glance, Gerard Manley Hopkins's *As king-fishers catch fire, dragonflies draw flame* might seem an odd choice to illustrate the sacredness of work. I had read the poem as an undergraduate English major. It hardly left an impression. Then, about five years ago, a colleague read the poem aloud at an awards luncheon for a group of Chicago businessmen called Business Executives for Excellence and Justice. I was struck by the line, *"What I do is me: for that I came."* Suddenly I could connect the dots, and I understood what Hopkins seemed to be saying about the sanctity of work. By that time, my own winding work journey had taught me a thing or two.

My conception of "good work" arose largely in reaction to my parents' work. When I was thirteen, my mother took a job in a pickle factory to help pay my tuition to a Catholic girl's academy. It was truly a "job." For eight hours a day she stood ankle deep in red rubber boots in a pool of gray water, hosing down cucumbers. I sometimes visited my mother at lunchtime. At noon, Sam Wachsburg, the factory's owner, would blow a plastic whistle. The women workers would scramble up a staircase to a small room, no bigger than a pantry. There, they'd squeeze against one another on a small bench, pull out their lunch sacks, and eat. They had to be fast. The whistle blew again promptly at 12:30, and it was back to work. The whole scene filled me with a combination of anger and shame.

My father also did manual labor. He drove a truck for forty years, rising at 3:30 in the morning to beat the traffic on the crowded New York–New Jersey highways. Once, he took me to his office, where his boss, the nephew of the company's owner, chewed him out for being a few minutes late. My father silently eyed his shoes as his boss continued the tirade. I couldn't have been more than five or six, but I remember vowing to myself that I would never let anyone treat me like that. Education would be my ticket out. Work, for me, would be something meaningful and exciting. "The use of all one's talents in the pursuit of excellence in a life affording scope" is how the Greeks defined happiness. That is what work would be for me.

My wish seemed to come true when, at the end of my senior year of college, the *Washington Post* hired me for a summer internship. My parents drove me to Washington in their beat-up Chevy Caprice. The Watergate scandal had made the paper famous; the *Post* represented every young journalist's dream job. I was one of only two interns who didn't come from an Ivy League school (I had graduated from tiny St. Peter's College, a Jesuit liberal arts school), so I pushed myself to be the best. At the end of the summer, I was one of only two interns the *Post* asked to stay on. I couldn't believe my good fortune. I threw my heart and soul into my work. I worked late nights and on weekends because I loved what I was doing. The problem was, all I did was work. I had no life. In my seventh year at the *Post,* I was hospitalized for exhaustion, malnutrition, and acute anemia. I was miserable and didn't know why. I was so clueless then; I thought my happiness would lie in getting an even better job with an even bigger newspaper. And I soon got my wish.

The *Wall Street Journal,* then the largest newspaper in the country, wanted to hire me. I was assigned to the Chicago bureau and worked with many fine journalists. But I soon lapsed into the same pattern, staying later than everyone else at the office, working weekends and holidays. Leaving the office around eight o'clock one Friday night in July, I spotted a street festival just a few blocks from the *Journal* office. A band played, people were dancing. I thought about stopping by but realized I'd look ridiculous lugging along my work files and wearing my dress-for-success clothes. So I went home and spent the evening alone. Even when I had plans, I let work intervene. I remember purchasing tickets to see Rudolf Nureyev dance. News broke on my beat the night of the ballet, so I missed that performance. I bought tickets for the next night. Same thing happened. On the last night of the performance, I again bought tickets. It was a Sunday evening, and a colleague and I were working on a front-page story for the next day's paper. When I said I was taking off early for the ballet, my colleague asked incredulously, "You're not going to leave *now,* are you?" So I stayed. I never got to see Nureyev dance in Chicago, or anywhere else. He died not long afterward.

The long work hours and the pressure I put on myself to succeed took an unseen toll. I was sinking deeper into depression, though I didn't know it then. I still managed to do my work and won eight awards for my writing in eight years. In 1993, I was a finalist for the Pulitzer Prize in feature writing. Every time I'd win an award, it would feel good for a few days, a week maybe; then the feeling would pass. There came a point, though, when I became so knotted up inside that my work began to suffer. I even questioned whether my writing talent had simply disappeared. I should have realized then that I needed a break—a sabbatical, something. In 1994, when the *Journal* laid me off in my second year in London, a door finally opened for change. The layoff was a devastating blow to my ego. But eventually, perhaps even grudgingly, I began to recognize an opportunity. This was a chance to do the things I had long wanted to do. And what I wanted was a life that included work, not work that happened to include a life.

I now look upon the day of my layoff as a kind of second birthday. My sense of identity no longer depends on what I do for a living, which is why the Hopkins poem resonates so deeply with me now. Just as kingfishers catch the light, dragonfly wings draw color, and tongs ring out the voice of bells, each person has a purpose to fulfill. That purpose is to reach the being that "inmost dwells," as Hopkins put it: our true and genuine self. *Do What You Love, The Money Will Follow* is the title of a popular book. Joseph Campbell would say, "Follow your bliss." That doesn't mean that everyone gets to work at his or her dream job. Hopkins himself struggled over his twin vocations as priest and poet. He thought one detracted from the other, and at one point even burned all his extant poems. "Slaughter of the innocents," he called it. He fretted over ever leaving anything of substance behind. "Birds build—but not I build," he wrote toward the end of his life. He called himself "Time's eunuch," who could "not breed one work that wakes." Yet Hopkins found consolation in the life of Alphonsus Rodriguez, a Jesuit lay brother, who had worked as a doorkeeper. Alphonsus was eventually declared a saint, but his sainthood, Hopkins says in a poem, was not "flashed off exploit." In other words, it doesn't matter what work we do. As Alphonsus proved, any job can become a vocation.

So often I hear of people who decide at midlife to leave their profession to go into some form of church work. To me, that narrows the definition of vocation. All work can be a form of ministry. (When Charley was state's attorney of McLean County, Illinois, he regularly referred to his work as chief prosecutor as ministry.)

Hopkins, good Jesuit that he was, firmly believed that all work, diligently and honestly performed, gives glory to God. Meditating on the Spiritual Exercises of St. Ignatius of Loyola, he wrote: "Smiting on an anvil, sawing a beam, whitewashing a wall, driving horses, sweeping, scouring, everything gives God some glory if being in his grace you do it as your duty. . . . To lift up the hands in prayer gives God glory, but a man with a dung fork in his hand, a woman with a slop pail, give him glory too. He is so great that all things give him glory if you mean they should."

When I think of my parents now, I realize they *were* successful. Perhaps not as the world defines success, but in the sense that they worked hard, raised their family, made ends meet, and lived honorable lives. My mother was a generous friend to the women she worked with. My father, when he owned his own truck, could have hired family members or friends to work with him. Instead, he gave jobs to men who needed them, often African Americans. In the 1940s and 1950s, my father was an equal opportunity employer before it became the law.

Another great Jesuit thinker, Teilhard de Chardin, saw our work in the world as carrying on the work of creation. He wrote: "We may perhaps imagine that creation was finished long ago. But that would be quite wrong. It continues still more magnificently, and at the highest levels of the world. . . . We serve to complete it, even by the humblest work of our hands."

"The humblest work of our hands." I love that thought. It reminds me that our real work is the work of compassion, of creativity, of leaning into the mystery that is found in each life. Whatever job we do, we can make it a work of the heart.

Juvenile Day

Charles Reynard

Like loaves and fishes, a miracle
to find one desultory day each week
amid traffic days, motions days,

felony days, here in Heart Break:
courtroom on the second floor,
the intersection of South Surrender

and West Submission, where
I sit and await with mumbled prayers,
the comings of those like Danny.

The law, in its due and majestic process,
assigns fault, sometimes responsibility.
There's a difference, I frequently say

from my bench-top Olympus, incanting
the fifteen minute legal liturgy called
Permanency Review, once every six months.

Wherefore, I find it is not your fault,
Danny, that you have Post-Traumatic
Stress Disorder, Oppositional Defiant

Disorder, and R-O bipolar illness.
Or that you are under the influence
of Depakote 500 mg, Zoloft 200 mg,

and Seroquel 40 mg. But it is
your responsibility not to swallow
shampoo or thumbtacks, not to run

away, steal gas, shoplift matches
from Dollar General, not to knife
your neighbor or your nurse during

the manic phase of your moon,
the unspeakable sorrow hidden
behind your chaotic chronicle

(which we cannot talk about because
you may break, Family Service says,
even though you are *doing better*).

Blessed son, I hold you in my hand,
so helpless to help, so blind to watch
over you in your garden of griefs.

A BOY NAMED DANNY
CR

MANY PEOPLE LOOK UPON their work as the dreary prose of economic necessity, not the romantic poetry of heroic mission. They live for quitting time, weekends, and vacations. They certainly see nothing inspiring, imaginative, or spiritual in their workplace roles. Judy and I are fortunate enough to have careers that do not trap us in deadening work. Thus, it may be inappropriate for us to say to others with more difficult working lives that the very ordinariness of work can be, and ought to be, a verdant source of spiritual growth. We will say it anyway.

For me, the legal profession has provided a deep well for spiritual hydration. I say this knowing full well that many people either have unequivocal contempt for lawyers or are mystified by what lawyers do. "How could you defend a criminal like that?" was the most frequent question I fielded when I was in private practice. Less overt are the questions surrounding law as a profession of greed.

One of my principal strategies for emotional survival has been to avidly collect lawyer jokes. One comedian tells the story of a lawyer and his wife on a Caribbean cruise. A storm suddenly whips the seas into a bucking frenzy, causing the ship to violently toss the attorney overboard. As he struggles to the surface, he notices sharks circling him. But then the sharks form two single file lines. They swim next to him to the side of the ship, where he is rescued. His wife says it was a miracle that the sharks didn't attack him. He replies, "My dear, they merely extended me professional courtesy."

Even my best friend, a farmer, added to my collection one morning when we went swimming at our local YMCA. He exclaimed, "It was so cold this morning!" then waited expectantly for me to ask, "How cold was it?" He grinned. "It was so cold I saw a lawyer with his hands in his *own* pockets!"

On the serious side, I've had friends question how I've coped with seeing so many heartrending cases as a prosecutor, defense attorney, and now judge. Courts collect people in crisis, victims of unspeakable acts, and moral ambiguities the way recycling centers receive the discards of a throwaway society. Many friends say they are glad they don't have to do this kind of work; I am equally grateful that I don't have to do some of their jobs.

My first assignment as a judge was in Livingston County, Illinois. I traveled every day from my home in Normal to Pontiac, the Livingston county seat. My courtroom was on the second floor of a well-preserved nineteenth-century courthouse. Pontiac is a small community—about 15,000 residents. But it is the largest municipality in Livingston; in geographic terms it is the third largest county in the state. I was one of just three judges who heard a wide range of litigation cases, from felony trials to estate settlements. As the judge with the least seniority, I presided over traffic and misdemeanor cases every day of the week except one. Tuesday was juvenile day.

The juvenile court hears criminal cases involving children under age seventeen, as well as the cases of those under eighteen who have been allegedly abused or neglected, those who are truant, or are otherwise in need of supervision. With only one day per week allocated to juvenile court, there were many weeks we could not respond to the overflowing needs of these young people, so we would encroach on the other schedules to hear these cases. A typical juvenile day might start out with the case of a fifteen-year-old vandal on drugs. Next up: a thirteen-year-old runaway who is having a lesbian affair with her thirty-year-old teacher. Then, the sexual abuse of a six-year-old girl by her mother's live-in boyfriend. In many ways, Tuesdays were the worst days of my week. Yet in other ways, they were the best.

"Danny's" case is illustrative. His case had navigated the system for almost three years when I was first assigned to it. Danny had entered the juvenile justice system at age eleven. His mother and various of her live-in partners were accused of abusing and neglecting him. His family could not handle his explosive behaviors. He was placed in foster care and failed in several placements. He ran away, took drugs, attacked his foster parents and siblings, and exhausted the energy of the teachers and caseworkers who tried to help. During the previous year, he had been placed in the secure psychiatric unit of a hospital two hours north of Pontiac. Doctors there medicated him with a bewildering array of psychotropic drugs. Yet he still periodically acted out with nurses, doctors, and fellow patients.

I conducted two six-month review hearings in Danny's case. After the first one, I held only the most remote hope for his improvement. He seemed destined for what we in the courts call "back-warding," technically, an indefinite hospitalization, though in reality a form of imprisonment. At the second hearing, caseworkers reported that Danny was doing better. His medication had been adjusted, and his destructive outbursts were less frequent. Caseworkers recommended continued hospitalization. The therapists believed that Danny was still so unstable that they were not yet able to address with him the psychological origins of his problems. Each time I met Danny in court I felt ill equipped to do more than mouth some fairly tepid bromides about doing his best to cooperate with the folks treating him. I probed service providers concerning the possibility of more hopeful approaches. But ultimately, I knew it would take a far higher power than the court to restore Danny's life to wholeness.

As a judge, I have the authority to dictate whether someone goes free or to jail, goes home or to the hospital, to supper or to death row. And yet, it astonishes me how utterly powerless I am to help people like Danny, who are suffering the worst kind of pain. Still, I show up each day, along with social workers, police officers, prosecutors, defenders, probation officers, interns, and volunteers of various stripes. I show up with hope. Hope that I might at least mitigate, if not resolve, some youth's or some adult's chronic misery. That is what keeps my work meaningful. That is what makes miraculous those grace-filled days when I'm able to see the smallest steps forward.

PART SEVEN
LOSS

KAMEHAMEHA DRIVE-IN,
25 YEARS LATER
Barbara Hamby

Aiea, sandwiched between Pearl Harbor and Waipahu, scene
      of my adolescence, soundtrack
by Bob Dylan via Jimi Hendrix, "All along the Watchtower,"
      those initial
chords vibrating still through my bones with the first
      rumblings of
desire, more romance than eros, and an urge to move
      away from Hawai'i, anywhere, somewhere
exotic, like England in the nineteenth century,
      having just seen
Far from the Madding Crowd at the Kam Drive-in, a perfectly cast
      movie, with Alan Bates as
Gabriel Oak, Peter Finch as Farmer Boldwood, and angelic
      Terence Stamp as Sgt. Frank Troy, before
heroin, drink, and chow stole their beauty
      and transcendence, and,
in what was probably her best role, except maybe *McCabe*
      and Mrs. Miller,
Julie Christie as the celestially christened Bathsheba Everdene,
      but I am immersed in a world of mangoes,
kimchi, plate lunches, nori rolls, li hing mui.
      My best friend
Lynn has Hodgkins disease, and when we meet, shows me her bald
      spot from radiation though she still looks like Ali

MacGraw but without the crooked tooth. Who has crooked teeth
      these days?
No one, as a matter of fact, but me. Lynn and I talk poetry
      and boys,
only I don't realize until later that no one is really talking
      poetry but me, but we're eating
popcorn and discussing metaphysics when Lynn and I go back
      to see Frank Troy walk into the sea
quivering with grief and cold, and I hardly know what it is
      to be cold, sitting on the hood of my Dad's old
Renault with the tropical sky moving like another film
      behind the screen,
seething with emotion so raw that I will run to the library,
      take up Hardy and his crew—
Tess, Jude, Eustacia Vye—and never let them go, forgetting
      how it all began
until 25 years later, looking for sushi take-out with my sister
      I see the marquee and remember the world of
VW vans and bugs, a world in which Lynn is still alive
      her flutey laugh echoing over palm fronds as
we gaze down the aisles of sputtering boxes at the cars
      filled with sleeping children, exhausted lovers in their
exodus from the drive-in, but we stay until the end, aimless,
      wild with being young in the
year of grace, 1969, that paradisal moment when we would
      see a movie, then go to
Zippy's or swim naked in the Pacific Ocean and imagine
      our endless lives beyond.

A SMALL COFFIN
JV

KERRY WAS A SKINNY, waiflike girl in my seventh-grade class. She sat in the last seat in the last row. I sat in the first seat in the first row—a place, to my solipsistic mind, befitting my position as one of the smartest, if not *the* smartest, kid in the class. Occasionally, I'd glance back at Kerry forlornly sitting there. She might as well have been in Africa. Kerry was not popular. She had frizzy hair and wore brightly colored jumpers and kneesocks the year the rest of us discovered miniskirts and fishnet stockings. Kerry had a harelip, though I doubt we even knew the word for it then. We thought she had a funny mouth. Kerry was absent more than any other student. When our teacher, Mr. Luppino, called on her, she rarely knew the answer. At one point he stopped calling on her altogether, I suspect to save her the embarrassment.

Kerry would have slunk into oblivion in the outskirts of class if it wasn't for her habit of arriving late for school nearly every day. We'd be forced to notice her as she creaked open the classroom door, removed her unfashionably colorful coat, and settled into her desk at the back. There was a part of me that felt sorry for her. But what made it hard to befriend Kerry was that she was often mean. She screamed at other students for no apparent reason. Once, during a game of punchball, she began hitting my best friend Merrill in a fit of rage. After that, I felt it best to let Kerry live in her self-imposed exile.

One morning Mr. Luppino, a stocky man with a perennially perturbed look, arrived in class seeming even more somber than usual. "I'm afraid I have some very bad news this morning, boys and girls," he said. "Your classmate Kerry won't be coming back to class. Kerry died this weekend." There was no gasp, no tears, just silence. What none of us had known was that Kerry suffered from a congenital heart disease. That was why she had been absent for several weeks before Mr. Luppino's announcement. I hadn't even noticed. Mr. Luppino said our class would attend Kerry's funeral on Tuesday morning. How could someone my age be dead, I wondered. *Grandparents* died. Merrill tapped me on the shoulder from behind. "He's just kidding," she said. "Kerry's going to show up late like she always does."

On Tuesday morning, we marched off to Kerry's funeral Mass at St. Henry's Church. I will always remember the sight of the long white candle and Kerry's coffin beside it. It was a small coffin, just about my size. I spotted a woman who had been one of our substitute teachers in a pew. Why would a teacher who hardly knew Kerry be there? Maybe there was more to Kerry after all.

I suspect there is a Kerry in just about everyone's life: the kid who didn't make it out of grammar school or high school or college when we did. The kid whose life was inexplicably cut short. For years I wondered, why Kerry? Why not Janet or Shelly or Linda or any of the other kids in class? Why not me? It still puzzles me how a merciful God would let something like that happen to Kerry. And I still don't have an answer to my question. I do know that looking at Kerry's coffin that day in St. Henry's had a profound effect on me. I realized that day, in seventh grade, that my life would not be endless.

In Barbara Hamby's poem, it is her friend Lynn who doesn't make it. The poem evokes the dreamy moodiness of adolescent girls. You can just picture the two of them reading each other Wordsworth over hamburgers at Zippy's diner, in love with actor Terence Stamp, imagining themselves as Julie Christie in *Far From the Madding Crowd,* believing they are the two most misunderstood people in the world. Lynn suffers from Hodgkin's disease. But when she shows her friend her bald spot from radiation, it's almost as if she is displaying a talisman. At seventeen, how could these girls envision anything worse than watching a movie in a drive-in theater on a summer night and swimming naked in the Pacific? How could they imagine anything but their "endless lives beyond"?

Kerry's death still haunts me but, I think, in ways that are good for me. I once tried to make a list of the things she had missed by dying so young. I thought of how she never got to sip a mocha latte inside a Starbucks on a chilly afternoon or stroll down the Champs-Élysées on Christmas Day. How she never saw human beings walk on the moon or looked up a quote on the Internet. How she never saw Mary Tyler Moore toss her wool beret in the air. How she never made love to a man. It still fills me with guilt when I think about this. But just as often, I'm filled with gratitude. Gratitude for what the narrator in the film *American Beauty,* speaking from the grave, calls our "stupid little life." Ever since I was a youngster,

I've been driven to make the most of my life, to take advantage of opportunities that presented themselves, to "make my own luck" when doors didn't just open. I wanted to be sure, as Mary Oliver puts it so well in her poem *When Death Comes,* that I didn't die "simply having visited this world."

I've made it a practice since childhood to stop in the middle of something I'm doing—daydreaming on a train ride, cooking a meal, taking a bath—and remind myself how lucky I am to be alive. Which is what I am doing right now, writing these words in a lovely wooded spot in central Illinois called Funk's Grove. It's mid-October and the sun is low in the afternoon sky, dribbling light onto the few remaining leaves, turning them golden-brown. I'm here with my felt-tipped pen and yellow legal pad because it is just too beautiful to be inside. I sometimes think I became a writer because it's a way of fixing experience in memory, of saying: I lived. When I think of Kerry, I'm grateful that I lived to tell her story. Someone has to live to tell the stories.

In the months following the September 11 terrorist attacks, the *New York Times* ran short vignettes on the people who perished in the twin towers—some 1,900 personal profiles. The stories told of each person's family life, his or her travels, hobbies, interests, and plans for the future. Although these articles were each just a few paragraphs long, they read like short novels. So many of those who died were on the verge of a major life change: a wedding, the birth of a child, a job promotion, a long anticipated vacation. Reading these articles, I came to realize more sharply than ever before that there is no such thing as an "ordinary" life.

When I think of my classmate Kerry, I often wish I could remember a single time I reached out to her in kindness. But I never did. These days, I try to let people know I love and appreciate them. Still, I fail often at my own rule. Years go by, and I lose contact with good friends because I'm too busy to call or write. Just this week, a friend of mine passed away—an early death from cancer. I had called him twice and left messages after I heard that the cancer had returned, but we never made contact. I was always going to call again, e-mail, write ... The point is not to be hard on myself but to try to do better in the future. "The art of losing's not too hard to master," Elizabeth Bishop asserts in her poem *One Art*. She describes losing her keys, her mother's watch, houses she loved, a continent where she lived. "None of these will bring disaster." It is only the loss of a person—a voice, a loved gesture—that can never be regained. In that case, Bishop reminds us, "It's evident / the art of losing's not too hard to master / though it may look like (*Write* it!) like disaster." I try to be mindful each day that life does come to an end, that each moment I have with the people I love is precious. For that, I have Kerry to thank.

PERENNIAL
Susan Hahn

So what if next year the deep pink burst
will not appear outside my door.
What if, after all the tending,

the IVs filled with said miracles—droplets
from the blood bags that reawaken your body,
ignite your mind—your face,
a blossom, will not appear outside my door?
Today, June peonies lighten my path—so what

if next year they do not come back? If
they do and you do not,
I'll hack them down with an ax—
that they dare reappear,
their spread petals wild tongues
screaming *SO WHAT?*

So What

IV

For a period of four years, Susan Hahn watched her mother die of cancer. It was a long, slow good-bye. Having experienced the sudden death of my mother, the hard shock of it and the regret I felt at not being with her to say good-bye, I've often wondered if it would have been better to know that her death was imminent. The answer is always the same. It doesn't matter if the loss is sudden or expected, the pain is just as sharp.

Susan was a great support to me when I was grieving my mother's death. Help at such times often comes from unexpected sources. I had known Susan only casually before then, from meeting her at poetry events. And yet she ended up calling me and consoling me more frequently than many of my longtime friends. It's as if once you've experienced that kind of loss, you become a member of a secret society. You instinctively connect with the other members of the club.

Susan told me that *Perennial* virtually wrote itself. It describes what she experienced one day coming home from the hospital to find a clump of pink peonies beginning to bloom along the side of her house. Were they mocking her? So it seemed. "I saw these peonies and I knew they'd be there next year and my mother wouldn't," she told me. "I knew nature had beaten me. No matter how hard you try to care for someone, to keep them from death, there comes a moment when you know no matter what you do, you'll lose that person."

The poem's internal rhymes and similar sounding words give it a kind of singsong, nursery-rhyme feel. "I'll hack them down with an ax," sounds like a line from the Brothers Grimm. Her collection *Mother In Summer,* which includes this poem, begins appropriately enough with a quote from Lewis Carroll:

The sun was shining on the sea,
    Shining with all his might;
He did his very best to make
    The billows smooth and bright—
And this was odd, because it was
    The middle of the night.

Often, when I was grieving the loss of my mother, I was aware of the sun shining outside while in my own interior world it was perennially night. Sometimes, I'd watch a few minutes of a TV sitcom or a film comedy. Nothing seemed funny. I wondered if I would find anything funny again. For many months after my mother died, I don't remember being aware of color. The world seemed shaded in only grays and browns. C. S. Lewis experienced some of the same feelings after the death of his wife, Joy Davidson Gresham. In his book *A Grief Observed,* he writes, "I see the rowan berries reddening, and don't know for a moment why they, of all things, should be depressing. I hear a clock strike and some quality it had before has gone out of the sound. What's wrong with the world to make it so flat, shabby, worn-out looking. Then I remember."

In high school, one of my teachers once pointed to a glorious day in early spring to illustrate the Resurrection. Green shoots were beginning to sprout on branches. Daffodils had bloomed. "If you want evidence of the Resurrection," she said, "just look around you. The whole world is renewing itself." Even as an adolescent I could detect the flaw in that reasoning. Yes, trees and flowers return, even weeds. Human beings do not. When someone dies, you come face-to-face with the reality that you will never touch that person's hand again, hear his or her voice, laughter. If we happen to be lucky enough to have a voice on an answering machine, we play it over and over. Where's the hard evidence that life continues beyond death, C. S. Lewis asked. He says he found "no answer. Only the locked door, the iron curtain, the vacuum, absolute zero."

Doubt set into his Christian beliefs. He railed against God. Susan rages similarly. Only she directs her anger at the natural world, its capacity for rebirth. In several poems in *Mother In Summer,* she interweaves the imagery of nature and her mother's illness. In one, she compares her mother's tumors to "violent" purple tulips that, like bruises under the skin, swell against an already cracked window. "I want to scream / at the thickening / grass to give me my mother / back," she writes. But she receives no solace from nature. Lewis recalls how he prayed "in desperation" for God to heal his wife. Later he prayed to overcome his grief. What do you find, he asked: "A door slammed in your face, and a sound of bolting and double bolting on the inside."

For a year after my mother died, I attended a grief support group. The facilitators were a wonderful mother-daughter team named Yolanda Ericson and Kris Hallowell. The first words I heard from Yolanda and Kris were "things will get better." But I was still at the "so what" phase. I couldn't believe I'd ever feel better. The first thing you have to do, they told me, is let yourself grieve. "It's hard," Kris said.

Each week we would come in, and Yolanda or Kris would ask us to say who it was we lost and how the person died. At first I thought this was stupid. Why pick at the wound every week? Eventually, I got what they were driving at. The more you speak out loud about the loss, the more accustomed to it you become. The initial shock wears off. It becomes part of your reality.

We left each week with homework to do, usually writing answers to some questions. One exercise I found particularly healing involved drawing "life graphs." In the first, we drew a time line of our life with the person we had lost. We went year by year, month by month, and put down all our significant memories of life with that person. It was a great exercise because eventually I came to see that I had enjoyed a full and rich life with my mother. It was also a way to see her as the true human being she was, full of grace and flaws. As C. S. Lewis came to accept his wife's death, he also came to a realization—death will eventually separate all lovers. It follows marriage as naturally as marriage follows courtship. It is part of the human condition. Lewis felt a change come over him.

He realized, as he writes so eloquently, that his relationship with his wife "had reached its proper perfection."

For the second graph, we set down the significant events of our own lives. That was an even more powerful exercise. Here, I could see all that had been good in my life, all I had accomplished. That was a source of comfort. But there in black and white was also what I had failed to do. Were there people I needed to make amends with? Were there dreams I could yet achieve? Thinking about this propelled me toward the future. There was indeed much yet to live for. It occurred to me that living, and living abundantly, was the best way to honor my mother.

Grieving the loss of a loved one is probably the ultimate desert experience. But it is an inevitable part of life. If we're lucky, it will spur us on to growth. A few months after my mother died, I attended a talk on All Saints' Day given by my friends Eileen Durkin and her sister Julie. They spoke of their father, who had died after a long, painful struggle with cancer, and how acutely they missed him. Julie said that one day after he had died, she simply knew her father was with her in the room. Not in the flesh or as a ghostly vision, but as a presence. He came to her as she heard a song he often sang to her when she was a child. Lewis relates something similar. At the very point he stopped wanting his wife back *right now* in the flesh, a remarkable thing happened. "She seemed to meet me everywhere . . . I don't mean anything remotely like an apparition or a voice. I don't mean even any strikingly emotional experience at any particular moment. Rather, a sort of unobtrusive but massive sense that she is, just as much as ever, a fact."

I now know exactly what C. S. Lewis meant, and what Julie sensed. I tell friends who've lost someone they love that, as hard as it seems at first, there comes a point when you stop feeling the person's absence and start feeling his or her presence. Susan Hahn told me that the year after her mother died, the pink peonies on the side of her house bloomed as if on cue, the second week of June. "I got into my car and I started driving over them," she said. "Then I stopped. I pulled the car back and drove it into the garage. Now when I see them I think, how can I be angry at such beautiful flowers?" Amen.

PART EIGHT

BODY AND SOUL

BODY & SOUL
Judith Valente

"When you enter the world, you come to live on the threshold between the visible and invisible."

John O'Donohue, Eternal Echoes

Imagine those moments
 after the soul leaves the body.
  Imagine the body's immense
loneliness: a manse suddenly
 shorn of its single boarder. A child
  banging its fists against the living
room window, begging for its mother
 to *Come back!*
  as the car jerks out of the driveway
—for all the child knows, forever—
 and there's that awful last glimpse:
  back of a head growing smaller, smaller
through the rear windshield.
 This is why we should stay
  close to the body after death,
the way we used to hold wakes, at home
 and around the clock, until the body adjusts
  to its noiseless status, widowed rooms.

The monks of St. Lleuddad labored
 to pinpoint the seat of the soul.
  Day and night, in a dank cellar

they sliced through blackening corpses,
    the abbot settling finally on the pineal gland:
        cross-section of cranial concavities,
disengaged from the grosser parts of blood.
    How does the soul disengage?
        Shoot like air from a depressurized cabin?
Drift through a cracked window
    like the musk scent of a summer house?
        Does it seep like runoff, spurt like blood
from a severed vein, or exit in stages,
    an actor drinking in final bows?

John O'Donohue says we should
    think of death not as the breath
        on the back of the neck,
but a companion with us since birth,
    benign doppelganger who knows us
        better than we know ourselves.
That's not to say
    we're like Schrödinger's cat,
        at once dead and alive—
but death we carry with us,
    close as the fine hairs caressing
        our skin. Of course, John is a theologian.
I prefer physics. Julian Barbour's concept:
    time, a continuous tableau of many
        different nows, each a single frame

passing an all-seeing lens,
    so the instant of me in my kitchen
        a few minutes from now,
stirring a can of Campbell's tomato soup
    for lunch in 2001 Chicago,
        rolls in simulcast
with Andy Warhol applying a splotch
    of fire-engine red to his soup labels
        in 1962 New York.
We are at once fetus and 44 years old,
    molting in the Big Bang
        and reading this poem.

Where does the soul go?
    Meister Eckehart was asked.
        Nowhere, the great mystic replied.
He believed an invisible world
    lies just inside the visible,
        which would suit me just fine
because there is so much of this world
    I'd miss and want to hold on to,
        like Nick at the N&G Grocery,
saying *Artichokes, we have artichokes*
    before I even ask, and
        Next year we go together to Greece;
Earl Grey tea and cinnamon scones;
    this afternoon sun, waving a yellow hand
        across my neighbor's balcony,

falling like a spotlight on the roof
    of the Chicago Historical Society
        where the Stars & Stripes
dance a samba with the wind;
    this snow, spread like steamed milk
        on the sidewalk beneath my window;
this red terry cloth robe I'm wearing:
    spiral note pad, No. 2 pencil
        stuck inside its pocket.

Searching for the Soul
IV

T HAT MORNING, I HAD awakened early. For some reason, I picked up the phone and called my parents in Plano, Texas. It was Sunday. I usually called my mother every other day, but somehow four days had slipped by, and I hadn't talked with her. It was a month before my planned wedding, and I was busy with preparations. Though it was still only 6:30 in the morning, I knew she would be awake.

My mother rose at 5:00 a.m. every day. Diabetes had weakened her legs, so she shuffled from her bedroom to the living room. There, she would plop down in a blue reclining chair and begin to pray. Not just any prayers, but a stack of written ones from small prayer books collected over the years. At 7:00, she tuned in to Mother Angelica's Eternal Word Television Network to watch the Catholic Mass. Only then, after a good two hours of prayer, would she be ready for breakfast.

I can only remember a handful of times that my father ever answered the phone. The telephone was my mother's domain. She kept the receiver strategically placed on a table next to her reclining chair. This time, my father answered. I asked him how he was doing, and he said fine. We made small talk for a few minutes, and I finally asked, "Where's Mom?"

expecting him to say, "Oh, she's just in the bathroom, she'll be here in a minute."

"She's in Plano Hospital," he said in a tone that didn't reveal much concern.

"Plano Hospital?" I knew my mother feared hospitals the way an alcoholic fears being alone with an open bottle of Scotch.

"She went into one of those deep sleeps, and I couldn't wake her." He was referring to a type of diabetic stupor my mother slipped into on occasion. "I called your brother around midnight, and he phoned for an ambulance."

I knew how much an ambulance ride would frighten my mother. All her life she went to great lengths to sidestep death. She rarely traveled on airplanes and avoided elevators and large crowds. For a period of months when I was a child, she slept on the living-room couch after having a premonition that she might die in her bed.

I didn't dial the hospital next, but called my oldest nephew to see if he could go and check on her. His voice cracked on the other end of the line.

"I just talked with the hospital," he said. "She died."

"She *died?*" I couldn't believe what I was hearing. She couldn't have. She wouldn't die before the wedding, I blurted out. What was she *thinking?* This was a woman whose prayers I believed had saved my life twice—once when I was an infant with such a high fever that our family doctor told her there was nothing more he could do, and again when I nearly bled to death after a tonsillectomy. What I was really saying was that this death didn't at all conform to how I imagined it would be. I had always pictured myself, when the time came, at my mother's bedside, holding her hand, comforting her, helping to ease her passage to the next life. But there was no final good-bye. Sometime around midnight, my mother had suffered a brain-stem stroke, one of the most severe types. She passed away six and a half hours later in her hospital bed in Texas while I lay sleeping in mine in Chicago.

There is an old Celtic belief that the soul does not immediately depart from the body at the time of death. At one time in Ireland, friends and relatives kept a constant vigil beside the body for hours after a death. They believed that the body, released of its single boarder, might be frightened and in need of company. I thought of that now. Was my mother's soul floating somewhere nearby, lonely and lost? Ridiculous as it seems, I remembered the film *The Fighting Sullivans*. In the final scene, the Sullivan brothers, all killed in the same sea battle, ascend into the sky on an invisible staircase, then disappear into the clouds, still wearing their Navy uniforms. I fell down on my knees in my living room and peered into the thick cumulonimbus clouds that covered Chicago that rainy September morning. I was looking for any trace of my mother's soul I could find. There was none.

I have been a Catholic all my life. From childhood, I have been taught to believe in something called a soul, something eternal: the unseen essence of a person. My religion teaches that Jesus died on the cross, was buried, and on the third day rose from the dead, conquering death for all time. "Death, where is thy sting?" St. Paul asked (1 Corinthians 15:55). I found my beliefs sorely tested against the undeniable reality of my mother's lifeless body lying in a pale blue coffin. Her eyes were closed ever so slightly, as if she were asleep. Her lips looked as if they could part at any moment and begin to speak. But her lips did not move. There was only stone-cold silence.

A few weeks after she died, I spotted, by accident, a drawing a high school student had made commemorating those who died in the September 11 terrorist attacks. It showed hundreds of human figures rising up from the top of the flaming World Trade Center in New York. The figures rose into the open arms of Jesus. I wondered about the magnitude of all those lives being snuffed out at once. Were their souls released all at once?

In the months that followed my mother's death and the tragedy of September 11, I embarked on a quest to find out as much as I could about what happens to the soul—if indeed there is such a thing as an indelible, everlasting spirit inside each of us. I explored what each of the major religions has to say. I talked with a Jesuit priest who is a medical doctor specializing in the care of terminally ill patients. I spoke with a rabbi, a Muslim imam, a Buddhist monk, even my mother's undertaker. For several months I met with a grief counselor, who believed she had experienced a taste of the afterlife when her doctors snatched her from the brink of death.

I found something of comfort in each of the religious traditions. I was especially interested in talking to Dr. Myles Sheehan of Loyola University Medical Center outside Chicago. Dr. Sheehan is both a physician and a Jesuit priest. He would know about death from a clinical standpoint. But I wondered, what did he also know, as a clinician, about the soul? Was there anything in his medical experience that supported his Christian beliefs?

Having observed many deaths, Dr. Sheehan said he felt more, not less, certain in his belief that there is something to each of us beyond the body that holds us. "A tremendous difference occurs in someone in just a short period of time after he or she dies," he told me. "To be scientific about it, the heart stops beating and there is no longer any circulation. So tissues die quickly. There is a sense that the life has gone out of the person. There is, as the Greeks would say, 'a substantial change.' The living substance has gone to dead substance. What is no longer there is spirit."

For another perspective, I turned to my friend Rabbi Ira Youdovin. In the Jewish faith, the soul is considered the "non-physical, non-material, God-like" quality infused in each person, Rabbi Youdovin said. I appreciated the Jewish practice of pinning a small ribbon to one's clothes. It evokes a centuries-old practice of wearing a torn cloth when someone dies, to show how death ruptures the fabric of our lives. Some Jews refrain from going to parties or even listening to music for a month after a loved one's death, and that made sense to me. I liked the ritual of sitting shiva, praying for seven days for the one who has been lost. In our death-averse culture, people are expected to pick up their lives again as quickly as possible. "Get back to normal" is the conventional wisdom. Except that "normal" doesn't exist after the death of someone close to us.

My friend Gen Kelsang Khedrub, a Buddhist monk, told me Buddhists don't believe in a soul per se. However, after the body dies, the highest form of our consciousness, what is called the "root" or "subtle" mind, continues on. Buddhists believe that relatives and friends should perform acts of kindness after a loved one has died. It will help ease the dead one's transition into the next life. Like the ancient Celts, Buddhists also believe it takes a period of time for consciousness to leave the body. They talk of the "eight stages of dissolution." That is why Buddhists traditionally wait a period of forty-nine days before holding a burial rite. It is believed the consciousness floats in a dreamlike intermediate state for at least that period of time.

Yusuf Hasan is a Muslim imam I had interviewed when I was doing a story about hospital chaplains. He works at the Memorial Sloan-Kettering Cancer Center in New York, offering prayer and solace to many cancer patients. I sought him out again after my mother died because he has another job: to wash and prepare bodies for burial. I took great comfort in something he said: he has often seen smiles on the faces of the dead. It echoed something that Whit Sloane, my mother's funeral director, had told me. I asked him what he sees when he looks down at a dead body. He told me, "You can look at individuals that have passed away, and that which made them unique is gone. You realize that all that remains is that which is organic. The part that counts has gone." He added: "I don't know of any funeral directors or embalmers who don't believe in the soul."

Ironically, I derived the most comfort from a woman who doesn't believe in the soul at all. Annie Laurie Gaylor is an atheist and a member of the Freedom from Religion Foundation in Madison, Wisconsin. For Annie, the soul is merely a kind notion human beings have invented to protect themselves from the terror of facing up to their ultimate demise. She quoted the philosopher Bertrand Russell. He said,

> I believe that when I die I shall rot, and nothing of my ego will survive. I am not young and I love life. But I should scorn to shiver with terror at the thought of annihilation. Happiness is nonetheless true happiness because it must come to an end, nor do thought and love lose their value because they are not everlasting.

"Happiness is nonetheless true happiness because it must come to an end." Annie told me she drew great strength from that line. She said that believing there is no life beyond helps her appreciate this life even more. Oddly enough, it was Annie, with her rock-hard insistence that there is no such thing as a soul, who was most responsible for reconfirming my belief in the soul. I found myself rebelling from my deepest core against her assertions. The idea that we are merely matter seemed to defy logic. In many ways, I feel closer to my mother in death than I did in her life. At the oddest times, I sense her presence. Sometimes it is just the way the sunlight drips in through my bedroom window and casts a shadow on the wall. At other times I feel it when I catch sight of a leaf dancing in the wind outside my fifteenth-floor window, or I spot a Kelly-green shamrock stuck to a cement sidewalk. I don't know how or why, but in those times, I know she is near.

Interestingly, I wrote *Body & Soul* a few months *before* my mother died, before I ever started on my soul quest. It was one of those strange coincidences in which I glimpsed my future in my past. ("Time present and time past / Are both perhaps present in time future, / And time future contained in time past," T. S. Eliot writes in *Four Quartets*.) The poem is a meandering meditation on the soul. I wanted those who read it to be able to follow my thought process from beginning to end. The impetus for it came from a few different places. The first was a series of lectures I attended in Chicago, given by Irish theologian John O'Donohue. In his book *Eternal Echoes,* O'Donohue poses an intriguing question: If our soul lives on after we die, where was it before we were born? I was fascinated by O'Donohue's story of the ancient Celts, who believed that our bodies grieve the loss of the soul, their mate in life. The first part of the poem spins out that idea.

I honestly didn't know where the rest of the poem would take me. Then I thought of the fact that throughout history, people have tried to pinpoint within the body the location of the soul. The monks of St. Lleudadd are characters from a novel I once read, but the type of experiments they engaged in, in search of the soul, have some basis in history.

After I began the poem, I spotted an article in a science magazine about physicist Julian Barbour's theories of time. I never took much science in college, but I find myself increasingly fascinated by biology, chemistry, and physics. Barbour theorizes that all time is eternally present. In that collapsible world, the present moment of writing this sentence coexists alongside, say, a public beheading in 1789 Paris, or Socrates peppering his disciples with questions in an ancient Athenian agora. I imagined all of these scenes from throughout recorded history rolling in simulcast on a wide-screen television.

The poem's ending plants itself firmly in the present and in the reality at hand: the grocer I routinely encounter, the view from my balcony, the bathrobe I wear when I'm writing, the notebook inside its pocket. It's my way of saying that the sacred, that which connects us to a life beyond, is nonetheless rooted in the everyday, in the stuff of life at hand. "Where does the soul go?" someone asked the thirteenth-century theologian Meister Eckehart. "Nowhere," he replied. Eckehart, one of the great mystics, believed an invisible world exists within the visible. And in that invisible world are the souls of all who have gone before us. We, the living, with our limited consciousness, simply don't have eyes to see them.

There is a postscript to this story. After my mother died, a dear man, the gardener at St. Michael's church in downtown Chicago, planted a rosebush in her memory alongside the church. Theresa was my mother's name, and St. Thérèse of Lisieux, known as "the Little Flower," was her favorite saint. My mother's rosebush bloomed in June. Then there were no more roses for the rest of the summer. On September 9, the one-year anniversary of my mother's death, I attended a Mass in her memory at St. Michael's. I decided to walk past the rosebush. There, on a bottom branch, bloomed a single red rose. It was as if my mother was telling me that she was all right. It was all right to go on with my life. It was all *all right*. It was as if those stone-cold lips I had stared at in her casket had finally decided to part, to speak.

The Idea of Ancestry

Etheridge Knight

1

Taped to the wall of my cell are 47 pictures: 47 black
faces: my father, mother, grandmothers (1 dead), grand-
fathers (both dead), brothers, sisters, uncles, aunts,
cousins (1st and 2nd), nieces, and nephews. They stare
across the space at me sprawling on my bunk. I know
their dark eyes, they know mine. I know their style,
they know mine. I am all of them, they are all of me;
they are farmers, I am a thief, I am me, they are thee.

I have at one time or another been in love with my mother,
1 grandmother, 2 sisters, 2 aunts (1 went to the asylum),
and 5 cousins. I am now in love with a 7-yr-old niece
(she sends me letters in large block print, and
her picture is the only one that smiles at me).

I have the same name as 1 grandfather, 3 cousins, 3 nephews,
and 1 uncle. The uncle disappeared when he was 15, just took
off and caught a freight (they say). He's discussed each year
when the family has a reunion, he causes uneasiness in
the clan, he is an empty space. My father's mother, who is 93
and who keeps the Family Bible with everybody's birth dates
(and death dates) in it, always mentions him. There is no
place in her Bible for "whereabouts unknown."

2

Each fall the graves of my grandfathers call me, the brown
hills and red gullies of mississippi send out their electric
messages, galvanizing my genes. Last yr/like a salmon quitting
the cold ocean-leaping and bucking up his birth stream/I
hitchhiked my way from LA with 16 caps in my pocket and a
monkey on my back. And I almost kicked it with the kinfolks.
I walked barefooted in my grandmother's backyard/I smelled the old
land and the woods/I sipped cornwhiskey from fruit jars with the men/
I flirted with the women/I had a ball till the caps ran out
and my habit came down. That night I looked at my grandmother
and split/my guts were screaming for junk/but I was almost
contented/I had almost caught up with me.
(The next day in Memphis I cracked a croaker's crib for a fix.)

This yr there is a gray stone wall damming my stream, and when
the falling leaves stir my genes, I pace my cell or flop on my bunk
and stare at 47 black faces across the space. I am all of them,
they are all of me, I am me, they are thee, and I have no children
to float in the space between.

I Am Thee

CR

THE RELATIONSHIP OF BODY and soul has engaged the greatest spiritual thinkers of every age. Plato thought of the soul as the essence of a person. St. John of the Cross believed that when we seek God wholeheartedly, the Holy Spirit breathes or *inspires* the soul with divine power. He likened this gentle inspiration to the breath of a breeze. In such a way, John believed, the soul of an ordinary person could achieve union with God. "This inspiration of the Holy Spirit into the soul, through which God transforms it, produces delights in it that are so sublime, so exquisite, and so profound that human language is incapable of describing them. And human understanding cannot perceive them," he wrote. In the twentieth century, the great Trappist visionary Thomas Merton said that to be fully alive is to live with the recognition that one is at once "body, soul, mind, heart, spirit."

Beyond even what my Catholic upbringing taught me about the existence of the soul, I have always had the visceral sense that there is more to our being than our physical body. Etheridge Knight's poem *The Idea of Ancestry* confirmed for me, more than any theological treatise, a real and practical sense of the soul. Knight finds in ancestry an unending connection to the soul. Perhaps because slavery tore asunder so many family lines, the "idea of ancestry" for many African Americans became more a matter of soulful connection than mere recorded history.

I first discovered Knight's work in *Poetry Speaks,* a wonderful book and compact disc collection of poets reading their own work. Judy and I were looking for poems to use in the poetry workshop we conduct once a month at the Cook County Juvenile Detention Center in Chicago. Knight published his early poems while confined to an Indiana prison. He had met and received guidance from the renowned African American poet, Gwendolyn Brooks. We hoped the students would identify with Knight, who wrote angrily, but always authentically, about his imprisonment.

Knight's life was inextricably woven into his idea of ancestry. He sits in his cell and mournfully gazes at the pictures on his wall of forty-seven members of his family. One wonders if the pictures were real photographs or whether some, or all, were images he conjured in his mind. Knight contemplates his own place in the constellation of family relationships. This gives him some measure of comfort. "I know / their dark eyes, they know mine."

We can imagine the longing he must have felt as his eyes scanned the ones with whom he had "at one time or another been in love." He focuses on the snapshot of a seven-year-old niece, "the only one that smiles at me." The only one, perhaps, whose gaze life had not yet hardened. We can do more than merely imagine his feelings. We can search our own store of photographs, the ones we keep in our wallets, on our walls, at our desks, or in the frail templates of our memories. In one of mine, my younger daughter is leaning her face toward mine as we cruise in a scuba boat on the Indian Ocean. In another, my older daughter and I are standing by a fountain at St. Mary's College in South Bend, Indiana, on the day of her graduation. Her face is filled with the anticipation of beginning her life's next chapter. In another, Judy and I hold hands in front of the statue of Atlas at Rockefeller Center in New York City, looking like two of the happiest people in the world. Each of these photos produces an overwhelming emotion. They give me a sense of grounded identity, a soulful connection to the people with me in the photographs.

Knight feels a similar connection to those he loves. "Each fall the graves of my grandfathers call me, the brown / hills and red gullies of mississippi send out their electric / messages, galvanizing my genes." And yet, for Knight, his crimes, his addictions, and his subsequent confinement also leave him with a sense of alienation. "I am a thief, I am me, they are thee." When he briefly reconnects with his family, he nearly beats his demons. "I walked barefooted in my grandmother's backyard/I smelled the old / land and the woods." There is a promise of salvation in community. But in a matter of time, his old habits return. There is that curious line, "The next day in Memphis I cracked a croaker's crib for a fix." I puzzled over what that line meant. One day, Chicago poet Li-Young Lee came to our poetry workshop at the detention center to read some poems. He had selected a few of Knight's poems because many of them share similarities with the type of rap lyrics the students love to listen to and often imitate in their own poems. He told me what the line meant.

Back in the seventies, Lee had been assigned to serve as Knight's driver when the poet gave a reading at Lee's college in California. Knight told Li-Young that when he was a burglar, he had vowed never to hurt anyone. He would read newspaper obituaries to scope out the addresses of dead people, "croakers," as he called them. Knowing the time and date of the funeral service, he could deduce with some degree of certainty when the croaker's home, or "crib," would be empty. He would then "crack" or burglarize it, looking for money, valuables, and drugs. When he went to prison, Knight became the empty space on the wall in the family album, like the uncle who went missing and whose dates are left blank in the family Bible. And yet, he feels a bond that cannot be broken as he looks at the forty-seven faces. "I am all of them," he concludes. "They are all of me."

Knight amplifies this theme in another of his well-known poems, *Belly Song*. When the youths at the detention center heard a recording of Knight's smoky baritone reading this poem, with rhymes and tonalities similar to rap music, they spontaneously burst into applause. In *Belly Song*, Knight extends the metaphor begun in *The Idea of Ancestry* and explores the soul connection between all people. The "sea" in the poem evokes the Atlantic Ocean and what historians refer to as the Middle Passage, the crossing of the Atlantic that was the middle part of an African's journey from homeland to slavery in America.

And I and I/ must admit that the sea in you
Has sung/ to the sea/ in me . . .

And this poem This poem
This poem/ I give/ to you.
This poem/ is a song/ I sing/ I sing/ to you from the
bottom
of the sea
in my belly
This poem/ is a song/ about FEELINGS about the Bone
of feeling about the
Stone of feeling
And the Feather of feeling . . .

And now, in my 40th year
I have come here to this House of Feelings to
This Singing Sea and I and I/ must admit that the sea
In me
has fallen/ in love with the sea in you because
the sea that now sings/ in you
is the same sea
that nearly swallowed you
and me too.

Recently I read a book excerpt that helped me see a new dimension to Knight's sense of these soulful connections. Physicists have theorized that not only are all living and material objects made up of infinitesimal particles of matter but we are all inextricably linked, one to another, through an unbroken chain of particles. We are literally connected to one another. We are distinguished by the density of our physical presence, but there is no true separateness. If such a theory is true, then the bond between all of us is physical as well as visceral and soulful.

The connections Knight talks about in *The Idea of Ancestry* extend beyond blood relations. When I read Knight's poetry, I am swept back more than thirty years to the time I taught about the Middle Passage as part of a black history class for seventh and eighth graders at St. Mel Elementary School on Chicago's west side. The first face that comes back to me is that of bright a African American student named Cannon.

When I met Cannon, Renetta, Alvin, Harold, Letitia, and the other remarkable students in this class, I had been a teacher for five years. Although I was paid to teach *them*, together we studied black history, criminal law, juvenile law, and urban law with the help of a social studies curriculum guide. Teaching provided some of the most memorable experiences of my life. Cannon was particularly remarkable. He was one of the shortest boys in the class, perhaps only five feet tall, surrounded by peers who had sprouted to over six feet. He was smart, a solid A/B student, but not the smartest. He nonetheless possessed a charisma that drew taller, stronger, smarter students to his side.

Cannon would often begin asking me a question with, "Uh hey, Ray-nard," deliberately drawing out the syllables of my name and flashing a sly, brilliant smile. Coming from another student, this behavior might have seemed disrespectful. But in Cannon it was not. He walked with a bold swagger. What represented posturing for other students, in Cannon marked a genuine buoyancy and self-confidence. Over the two years

I taught Cannon and the others, we held mock trials, built cardboard cities, and even did poetry-writing exercises from Kenneth Koch's book *Wishes, Lies, and Dreams.* The students wrote some truly remarkable poems. I was excited every day to arrive at school and be a part of this community of learners.

Life was tough for Cannon and the others. Once one of my students showed me a circular scar on his forearm; a former classmate at a public school had shot him. This boy occasionally needed a ride home, which I or one of the other teachers gave him so he could avoid aggressive recruiting by neighborhood gang members. Yet he and Cannon and many of the other students were fortunate enough to have parents committed to their children's success in school. Most of these parents were not even Catholic, yet they scrimped every penny to pay the tuition.

I left St. Mel a year after Cannon's graduation, in June 1974, to practice law. A short time later, I moved away from Chicago to central Illinois. Over the years I found myself wondering about Cannon. I occasionally checked the Chicago phone book at our local library to see if his name was listed. I would sometimes pop his name into an Internet search engine. I was unable to locate him. I searched for Cannon because I had this sense that he too was part of my ancestry, not the physical, blood relational kind, but a spiritual, soul ancestry that was integral to my growth as a human being.

Just this past year, after reading Knight's poems and feeling the wave of emotion they caused, I began searching again for Cannon. This time I located him. Cannon was living in the Chicago suburbs. When I phoned him, he was stunned to hear my voice after all those years, but remembered me right away. We agreed to meet one Saturday at a restaurant near his home. I confess to a great deal of apprehension. The last time I had seen him, I was twenty-six years old, exactly twice his age. Now we would meet as peers, two men in middle age. Would we still like each other? Would we even recognize each other? He was a slightly pudgy fourteen-year-old the last time I saw him. I had changed, too. Gone was my bushy seventies-style beard. My dark brown hair had thinned and turned silver.

Despite the decades of aging, we spotted each other even before we got out of our cars. The boy I had dubbed the most likely to succeed had indeed become a respected trainer at a major automobile corporation. He had broken down some racial barriers in the process. He was still a bachelor in his forties, but in a relationship that seemed to be working. He wore the same sly grin. And when he smiled, it was the young student of thirty years before who looked at me from across the space of time. We laughed and joked for an hour or so. I shared with him some of my professional successes, and personal disappointments. He shared his. Our connection had held.

While I don't want to overly romanticize this sense of connection, as I clasped his hand to say good-bye, I did feel a kind of wholeness. I felt I was experiencing both body and soul. I now think of the soul as not just a concept but an intimate reality, whole and inseparable from the body. Body and soul link us to the entire human family and to the divine. Knight's idea is that we are one, though our individual bodies may seem separated by various forms of imprisonment. For me, it is a comforting idea, one that offers spiritual sustenance for the harsh fragmentation we can encounter in life. The idea of ancestry is another way of saying that we are family. Or, as Etheridge Knight says, "I am all of them, / they are all of me."

PART NINE

MYSTERY

Star Turn

Charles Wright

Nothing is quite as secretive as the way the stars
Take off their bandages and stare out
At the night,
                    that dark rehearsal hall,
And whisper their little songs,
The alpha and beta ones, the ones from the great fire.

Nothing is quite as gun shy,
                                    the invalid, broken pieces
Drifting and rootless, rising and falling, forever
Deeper into the darkness.
Nightly they give us their dumb show, nightly they flash us
Their message and melody,
                                    frost-sealed, our lidless companions.

THE MYSTIC EYE
IV

EVERY ONE OF US is a mystic. We may or may not realize it; we may not even like it. But whether we know it or not, whether we accept it or not, mystical experience is always there, inviting us on a journey of ultimate discovery."

My late friend Brother Wayne Teasdale wrote those words in his book *The Mystic Heart*. Wayne was a self-described "monk in the city." He believed a person didn't need to seclude himself or herself in a monastery to live the contemplative life. In fact, Wayne considered the heart of the city an excellent place for a monk. Where is the need for contemplation greater? Because of his interfaith work, Wayne traveled often to far-flung countries like South Africa and India, though he despised flying. I once asked him how he handled such long flights. "I turn the whole flight into a meditation," he said.

Each of Charles Wright's poems is like a meditation. Simone Weil once called prayer "absolute unmixed attention." You find that same prayerful sense of attention in Wright's poetry. He writes about the inner life of inanimate things, the mystery inside the universe, what the writer Josef Sudek referred to as "the seventh side of the dice." Wright called his poetic efforts a search for "the still small center of everything."

Star Turn was one of the first Charles Wright poems I ever read. It made me want to run out and read everything else he had written. Here was a writer who saw with an inner eye, who reached deeply within himself. I wanted to go where he went. The soul is one of his major preoccupations, along with the past and the delicate dance between the here and now and eternity. "Wherever you are is a monastery," Wright once wrote. I found myself reading and rereading his lines, puzzling over them, pondering them. Lines like the one from his poem *Arkansas Traveller,* in which Wright describes the past as "a bright tweak at the vanishing point, blue on blue."

In the poem, *To Giacomo Leopardi in the Sky,* Wright considers the soul. He uses a wonderful word, *apotheosizic,* to describe the soul. It means "glorifying." He asks the intriguing question, "What if the soul indeed is outside the body / a little rainfall of light?"

A warning: Wright's poems are not easy. With their heightened language, unusual metaphors and startling images, they can seem like slow work through sand. An experienced poetry editor once said of Wright, "Sometimes I have no idea what the poem means, but the language is so original, I want to keep reading." The work cries out for a type of *lectio divina,* a process of "sacred reading" contemplatives use to break open a Scripture passage. First, you read the words, then you begin a process of meditation and reflection, going deeper and deeper into the heart of their meaning until you reach a kind of contemplative understanding you hadn't experienced before. Wright's work reminds us that there is a level to this life that lies beyond the circumference of daily routine. We walk between "eternity on one side and the daily landscape on the other," he once said.

Star Turn contains just such imaginative leaps. Wright compares the stars to a person who has been blinded and removes his bandages in hope of seeing the light. The stars open their eyes to find the night sky, a "dark rehearsal hall," where they can whisper their little songs in a sort of dumb show for those of us watching below. He leaves us with a haunting image of stars as lidless white eyes, our "frost-sealed . . . companions."

Once, I took an evening stargazing tour on a Hawaiian island. As we peered through telescopes at the moon's milky surface, our guide told us that astronomers have documented one-hundred billion galaxies in the universe. "A hundred billion!" I remember thinking that this fact alone ought to be proof of God. She told us the stars we saw were a million or more years old. Years later, when I came across Wright's poem, I thought of that, and it made his description of the stars seem all the more accurate: "invalid, broken pieces / Drifting and rootless, rising and falling, forever / Deeper into the darkness."

When I was a *Wall Street Journal* reporter, I went on an assignment to Utah, to witness the firing of a space shuttle solid rocket booster. One of the managers of the shuttle program at the time was a former astronaut, a man who had traveled to the moon. That evening, we ran into each other while we were both out taking a walk a few miles from the test site. The stars were just coming out. As night deepened, they looked like glittering bits of crystal tossed upward into the dark sky by some unseen hand. The prominent constellations stretched out above us: Orion, the Big Dipper. Here was a man who had traveled as close to these stars as a human being can get. Yet he was no less awestruck than I as we stood there looking up at the stars from our small patch of earth. He and I were two small particles standing still for a moment in the vastness of an inscrutable universe.

I'm not certain if that is the same feeling Charles Wright experienced in writing *Star Turn*, but I imagine I'm not far off. Though Wright attended an Episcopalian boarding school as a teenager, there is little evidence that he's a particularly religious man. My sense from reading interviews he's given is that he doesn't care much for institutionalized religion. But I have to believe that a person who writes as he does must possess a deeply spiritual core. Of God, he's said: "I don't think he exists other than in a harmony, the geometry and physics of whatever it is that holds the universe together." He has called God "the air we breathe . . . the metaphor for metaphor." Wright's poems, no matter their subject, are always trained on the great mystery at the heart of everything. I think that's a good way to live. For years now, I've made it a practice to witness the celestial events that occasionally occur. I set my alarm for 3:30 in the morning so I could watch a rare meteor shower spread across the Midwest in the fall of 2002—a wild ballet of light, the likes of which we won't see again until 2044. The summer that Mars passed more closely to Earth than usual, I woke up every morning before dawn to gaze up at the planet, a red bulb hung in a cobalt sky. I try to catch every lunar eclipse. Each time, I feel myself tapped on the shoulder, as if by a rod through which the supernatural flows. Each time I sense a true connection between my small self and that expansive, light-filled mystery that makes us dream of God.

The Panther

Rainer Maria Rilke
Translated by C. F. MacIntyre

His sight from ever gazing through the bars
has grown so blunt that it sees nothing more.
It seems to him that thousands of bars are
before him, and behind them nothing merely.

The easy motion of his supple stride,
which turns about the very smallest circle,
is like a dance of strength about a center
in which a mighty will stands stupefied.

Only sometimes when the pupil's film
soundlessly opens . . . then one image fills
and glides through the quiet tension of the limbs
into the heart and ceases and is still.

THE STORY OF DARLENE
CR

D ARLENE IS A MEMBER of the small faith group I meet with regularly for prayer. One day, I mentioned to Darlene that I was putting together a poetry anthology on the theme of finding the sacred in the everyday. I thought she might be interested. Darlene occasionally attends a poetry workshop at our local library sponsored by *RHINO* magazine. Her eyes lit up, and she immediately suggested *The Panther* by Rainer Maria Rilke. I had read Rilke's work in college, but didn't recall this poem. Darlene told me *The Panther* moved her deeply. It reminded her of the connection between the seen and unseen and of the marvelous mystery that sometimes allows us to sense what can't be measured or proved. At that time, I didn't know Darlene's story. That would come later.

A few days after our chat, Darlene sent me a translation of *The Panther*. The poem left a powerful impression. I had imagined the panther, in nature, to be a near-perfect expression of freedom, strength, and distilled beauty. Rilke's panther, however, is caged, capable of seeing only "thousands of bars" and darkness beyond them. He strides in circles. Despite his strength, his "mighty will stands stupefied." The poem reminded me of the limits imposed on our consciousness as part of the human condition.

In his book *Awakenings,* Dr. Oliver Sacks describes a group of patients who suffer from post-encephalitic Parkinsons, a disorder that freezes them in sometimes decades-long periods of sleep. One of the patients is Leonard Lowe, portrayed by Robert De Niro in the film version of the book. At age forty-six, Leonard was speechless and almost completely without voluntary motion. But he could spell out messages on a small letter board. Sacks asked Leonard, "What's it like being the way you are? What would you compare it to?" Leonard spelled out "Caged. Deprived. Like Rilke's 'Panther.'"

And yet Rilke's poem seems also to suggest that there's a way to overcome the blindness, to look beyond the dailiness of existence and see through to moments of transcendent beauty. Certainly for Leonard, who had been stuck for years in a comalike state, every moment of conscious existence seemed transcendent. In our information-driven world, we tend to focus on objective reality, composed of data. We view it as the *only* reality. Yet, just as certainly as we walk and breathe, we live within the heart of a mystery. C. S. Lewis called this the *real* real world. It lies just beyond the conscious world, in the same way the conscious world lies in wait just outside Leonard's comatose state. These are the moments when "the pupil's film / soundlessly opens" and awareness "glides through the quiet tension . . . / into the heart." At times like these, we don't so much see as sense; we don't so much know as intuit.

I found myself thinking a lot about the Rilke poem. And yet, my interpretation of the poem seemed inadequate, too cerebral. I felt confined, somewhat like the panther, turning in circles, unable to achieve clarity and understanding. The camera-like opening of my pupils came later, when I learned the entirety of Darlene's story.

Several weeks went by after Darlene sent me the poem. When we caught up again at our small faith-group liturgy, I visited with her at our host's dining-room table. As we nibbled on some cookies and fudge, I asked her how she was doing. She had seemed a little distracted, perhaps tired. Initially, she said she was fine. Then she shared what must have taken considerable courage.

"Actually, now I am doing a little better," she began. "I've been in the hospital with depression. It's been really rough." Darlene ordinarily speaks in a rather clipped, plainspoken fashion. It occurred to me that she might be controlling her expression while trying to gauge my reaction.

"I'm sorry to hear that. Are you getting back on your feet?" I asked. It was a bit bewildering to figure out what to say after someone shares something so painful. It reminded me of the Eric Berne title, *What Do You Say After You Say Hello?*

Darlene said the hospitalization had been absolutely necessary, though it had been a traumatic experience. She had felt profoundly isolated. "Why I never figured out I should ask this group for help," she said, pausing to look in the general direction of the other members in the next room, "I just don't know."

It was soon time to leave. What I should have done, as a friend, was call Darlene sometime that week and suggest coffee and conversation. I guess I was struggling to figure out how to best be her friend. I eventually did call and invited her for breakfast on a Saturday morning to talk about *The Panther* and what the poem meant to her. As we ate our eggs, I asked if her experience of depression was similar to the sort of confinement the panther suffers.

Darlene is a mental health counselor by trade. She said she had not thought of it in that way. "Depression is essentially a chemical imbalance," she explained, somewhat wearily, as if she had tried to express this to countless others in the past. Her depression required medication and therapy. I realized I had oversimplified her situation, unwittingly compressing it into a stereotype. I apologized and asked if she would tell me more about it.

"I first got treatment ten years ago." To her, it was ironic that, as a highly trained mental health service provider, she instantly would have recognized the symptoms in one of her clients. She dealt with her own symptoms largely by denying their existence. She felt that as an employee of a mental health agency, she simply could not afford to *have* a mental illness. She couldn't bear the thought of needing psychiatric services. She feared becoming a "high maintenance" employee in the eyes of her employer. She thought it would cost her her job.

Meanwhile, the depression advanced like a burgeoning shadow. She felt so listless that she slept during most of her off-work hours. She sometimes sneaked a catnap at work. Still, she devised a litany of excuses for not seeking help. In her words, "I kept pedaling faster and faster." She later recognized that she used her work with her clients as a means of distancing herself from her own needs.

When she reached a breaking point, Darlene finally told the doctor with whom she worked that she needed help. She asked him to treat her as a patient in his private practice. Still struggling with denial, she let another year pass before she actually started treatment.

The first weeks and months of the treatment were difficult. The doctor began the long process of determining which medications would work best, while adjusting their levels to respond to side effects. Even with medication, Darlene did not know whether she would be able to find ultimate relief. Her life seemed like an endless list of tasks, all too complicated to master. She fought what must have been a terrifying battle. Only after we had talked a long while did she reveal that before getting treatment she had actually planned how to get hold of a friend's gun to shoot herself. She even decided where she would do it. Those suicidal thoughts diminished, but she occasionally imagined driving her car into a wall as a way to end her pain.

As she related her story, the image of the caged panther became all the more powerful. His sight, like her inner sight, had grown "blunt" from peering through bars. She used the word in the clinical sense of "blunted affect," a deadening of expression. Feelings of isolation and unworthiness churned inside of her in an obsessive dance, like Rilke's panther treading over and over the small circle of his cage. "A mighty will stands stupefied."

About a year ago, Darlene faced another crossroads. By then she had ingested an array of psychotropic medications over a nine-year period. One pill elevated mood, another controlled anxiety, another kept her from sleeping during the day, and so forth. However, there were the side effects. Were the pills poisoning her in one or more ways? She confronted a future of thirty, forty, perhaps fifty more years of drug therapy. She questioned whether her liver could endure the pharmaceutical assault.

Darlene consulted with her psychiatrist and psychologist. Both advised against discontinuing drug therapy. They informed her that the decision to go off medication would be hers. A little more than six months after discontinuing her drug regimen, Darlene said she knew again she was in trouble. She had trouble coping with everyday life, "one layer after another," as she described it. She called her doctor and said simply, "I made a mistake."

Darlene restarted her medication. Nonetheless, she had to be hospitalized. The experience was tortuous. She was placed with patients who were far more out of contact with reality than she was. She contemplated, with no small measure of anger, what she felt was the patronizing air of one of the counselors who asked in a class session, "Raise your hand if you have ever had a need to communicate." It was only after two subsequent hospitalizations that she realized it was her illness that had spurred those angry reactions in her, not anything that particular counselor, who wound up being one of her best supports, did or didn't do.

Darlene is now out of the hospital. She has taken up anew the daily struggle to stay alive. Her most recent challenge involves a revised diagnosis. Because of her anger symptoms, her psychiatrist has diagnosed her as suffering from bipolar disorder. While she struggles emotionally to accept her diagnosis, she must now physically adjust to a whole new regimen of medications.

And yet she has hope. Every once in a while, she explained, hope appears as if in a snapshot, like the instant the panther's eye soundlessly opens. In those moments, she is aware of the simple beauty of the ordinary world, and of the beauty and goodness inside herself. At those times, hope "glides through the quiet tension." Darlene puts her fist to her heart. Her eyes moisten. "I know the words don't adequately translate this . . . this *relief!*"

I started by saying that Rilke's panther seemed to me to be a metaphor for the human condition and the profound sense of confinement we can experience. Darlene's story puts flesh on the poem for me. It is no longer a mere cerebral exercise. Yet it remains a mystery to Darlene, and to me as well, how we come to be inside these cages. Equally mysterious is that we can, and do, get out of our cages. At a recent poetry presentation, Judy discussed the work of Jalāl ad-Dīn ar-Rūmī, a thirteenth-century poet and mystic who was born in what is now Afghanistan. Rumi's poetry enjoyed a particular resurgence in the wake of the September 11 terrorist attacks, perhaps because so much of it invites us to reach beyond the obvious, beyond the confines of the human condition. After a point, reason fails us, and we must give ourselves to mystery. In one of his most famous poems, *The Guest House,* Rumi compares being human to an inn where joy, delight, shame, and depression are travelers. The poet's advice: "Welcome and entertain them all."

PART TEN

PRAYER

The Hammock
Li-Young Lee

When I lay my head in my mother's lap
I think how day hides the star,
the way I lay hidden once, waiting
inside my mother's singing to herself. And I remember
how she carried me on her back
between home and the kindergarten,
once each morning and once each afternoon.

I don't know what my mother's thinking.

When my son lays his head in my lap, I wonder:
Do his father's kisses keep his father's worries
from becoming his? I think, *Dear God,* and remember
there are stars we haven't heard from yet:
They have so far to arrive. *Amen,*
I think, and I feel almost comforted.

I've no idea what my child is thinking.

Between two unknowns, I live my life.
Between my mother's hopes, older than I am
by coming before me, and my child's wishes, older than I am
by outliving me. And what's it like?
Is it a door, and good-bye on either side?
A window, and eternity on either side?
Yes, and a little singing between two great rests.

Between Two Great Rests
CR

I HAVE ALWAYS STRUGGLED WITH prayer. Rote prayers leave me cold. Because I am rather shy, praying in community doesn't come naturally. Poetry, then, has frequently been for me a springboard for prayer. Li-Young Lee's poems bear a quietness and reverence that have always felt to me like prayer. I spotted *The Hammock* in a 2001 issue of *Poets & Writers*. The small faith group I belong to was scheduled to meet about a week later. I typed up the poem on decorative paper and made copies for everyone. I keep the poem taped to the side of a file cabinet in my home office.

Singing is one of the few ways I feel comfortable praying, and our small faith group is one of the few places I feel comfortable singing. So I was attracted to the line in the poem where Lee compares our lives here on earth to "a little singing between two great rests." It made me think of what a joyful, peaceful interval our Sunday night get-togethers have become in my otherwise hectic, complicated life.

I try to use my prayer time to give thanks. When Lee describes his mother singing to herself as his head lays hidden in her lap, I recall with great gratitude my own mother, Helen Rizzoli Reynard Phoebus. I remember well her daily burdens as a divorced mother with primary custody of her son. Though she was the beneficiary of a child support order of $10 a week, not a generous allowance even in 1953, my father, for all his other worthwhile traits, never paid her a dime of it. My mother didn't complain. She worked the third shift as a hospital nurse, hiring a babysitter to watch me at night. That way, when I woke up for school in the morning, she was home to cook me breakfast, usually an egg, two strips of bacon, and a slice of toast. Though she never expressed it, I know she worried for and about us.

When Lee speaks of a father's kisses for his own son, my thoughts go naturally to my two daughters. When she was in the second or third grade, Rachel gave me a birthday card she'd colored herself. On it, she had written in bright crayon that she loved me so much her heart "oh most burst." My heart "oh most burst" these many years later thinking about that card. Among my proudest possessions is a series of paintings that my younger daughter Meghan gave me from her gallery exhibit at Wellesley College. I have framed and hung each one of them in my living and dining rooms. The painting that makes me smile most is of an old ratty pair of my wingtips, hanging precariously from the edge of a table by their shoestrings. When I think of my daughters, I want, like Lee, to exclaim, *"Dear God"* in appreciation of my great good fortune. I sometimes even remember to say, *"Amen."* These are among my finest moments of prayer.

For Lee, the essence of prayer is to appreciate that our lives spin out between two great unknowns: what we were before our birth and what we will become after our death. Prayer is, in a sense, the connective tissue between those two unknowns. The poem reminds us to take joy in our simplest memories. Memories of mother, father, and our family of origin give us perspective on our beginning, even the unknown aspect of it that transpired before our birth. Contemplating our children, now that we have replaced our own parents, as Lee does in the poem, leads us to the opposite threshold, the point of our life's ending. Picture two trees on either side of eternity. Suspended in between is an ordinary hammock, the space where we live out our lives.

I met Li-Young Lee for the first time when he presented some poems at a workshop Judy and I facilitate for the young people in the Cook County Juvenile Detention Center. He confessed that he did not truly sense the full meaning of his poem until long after he had written it. It came to him one day halfway through a public reading: how the profoundly ordinary is juxtaposed with the profoundly unknowable. To approach this mystery became for him an act of prayer. He was not talking about traditional prayer as an outward expression directed toward an exterior God, whether the communication involves giving thanks or presenting a petition for God's guidance. He meant transcendent prayer, one that acknowledges the divine within our human existence, the "singing between two great rests."

About twenty students were present for the workshop that day, all between the ages of fourteen and sixteen. Most were accused of having committed a violent crime. Some faced first-degree murder charges. The students listened in rapt silence, if not complete understanding, as Lee read several poems. He told them that poetry is hard work because it demands that they move beyond the reality of being fourteen, fifteen, or sixteen-year-olds. Their challenge is to search for their *other voices,* those they can find in their distant pasts, in the thousands of years of collective experience we share as human beings. Wow! You could see these kids' eyes open wide with astonishment. Neither they nor I, for that matter, had ever thought about being a speck on humanity's long time line, or about sharing in the wisdom of ages past.

"Poetic effort is very complex," Lee explained.

> It has to do with breathing in and breathing out, which is really about living and dying. When we inhale, we are taking in oxygen and essential nutrients, infusing those nutrients into our organs, giving ourselves color and life. We are literally coming alive. On the other hand, when we exhale, we give away our nutrients, deplete ourselves a little of the life substance that sustains us. When we breathe out, we are, in a real sense, dying. When we speak, when we give our poems to others, we are literally giving our lives away, we are dying.

Lee suggested that this is what makes the sharing of poems so sacred.

One of the girls piped up that she didn't want to read her poem aloud at the workshop if it meant giving up essential nutrients. We all had a good laugh. But I knew the students were beginning to get the point. Yes, of course, Lee explained, she would be giving away something vital. But, he assured her, "As we give away our words with our breath, we are also receiving nutrients through our ears!"

Leaving the workshop that day, Lee dropped his head for a moment. "We will always have prisons, won't we?" he asked. With all my years of working in the criminal justice system as a defense attorney, prosecutor, and judge, I still found myself ashamed to admit that I had always taken for granted that this would be so. Yet something in his rather naïve question caused me to challenge my own hardened, supposedly realistic assumptions. If I can't even envision a world without prisons, then I am confined to a prison of limited expectations. I am unable to find the sacred right in front of me, inside the boy who wrote a poem about the terrified souls that the bricks in his cell block see nightly. Nor will I be able to see the sacred in the girl who wrote about keeping secret her rape at the age of twelve.

Lee said he hoped poetry would help these young people tap into the "voice of wisdom" inside of them. Perhaps then they could find a path away from violence, from self-destructive patterns of living. It's a long shot, I thought, though not a pipe dream. Poetry could well be the "hammock" connecting their sterile, bricked-in world, with the boundless sacred place inside them longing to be explored. I prayed that day a rare prayer of petition. I prayed that these troubled youngsters would experience the truly transcendent power of prayer and poetry. I prayed that poetry would lead them to "a little singing between" their "two great rests."

INSTRUCTIONS TO PAINTERS & POETS

Lawrence Ferlinghetti

I asked a hundred painters and a hundred poets
how to paint sunlight
on the face of life
Their answers were ambiguous and ingenuous
as if they were all guarding trade secrets
Whereas it seems to me
all you have to do
is conceive of the whole world
and all humanity
as a kind of art work
a site-specific art work
an art project of the god of light
the whole earth and all that's in it
to be painted with light

And the first thing you have to do
is paint out postmodern painting
And the next thing is to paint yourself
in your true colors
in primary colors
as you see them
(without whitewash)
paint yourself as you see yourself
without make-up
without masks
Then paint your favorite people and animals

with your brush loaded with light
And be sure you get the perspective right
and don't fake it
because one false line leads to another

And then paint the high hills
when the sun first strikes them
on an autumn morning
with your palette knife
lay it on
the cadmium yellow leaves
the ochre leaves
the vermillion leaves
of the New England autumn
and paint the ghost light of summer nights
and the light of the midnight sun
which is moon light
And don't paint out the shadows made by light

for without chiaroscuro you'll have shallow pictures
So paint all the dark corners too
everywhere in the world
all the hidden places and minds and hearts
which light never reaches
all the caves of ignorance and fear
the pits of despair
the sloughs of despond
and write plain upon them
"Abandon all despair, ye who enter here"

And don't forget to paint
all those who lived their lives
as bearers of light
Paint their eyes
and the eyes of every animal
and the eyes of beautiful women
known best for the perfection of their breasts
and the eyes of men and women
known only for the light of their minds
Paint the light of their eyes
the light of sunlit laughter
the song of eyes
the song of birds in flight.

And remember that the light is within
if it is anywhere
and you must paint from the inside
Start with purity
with pure white
the pure white of gesso
the pure white of cadmium white
the pure white of flake white
the pure virgin canvas
the pure life we all begin with

Turner painted sunlight
with egg tempera
(which proved unstable)
and Van Gogh did it with madness

and the blood of his ear
(also unstable)
and the Impressionists did it
by never using black
And the Abstract Expressionists did it
with white house paint
But you can do it with the pure pigment
(if you can figure out the formula)
of your own true light
But before you strike the first blow
on the virgin canvas
remember its fragility
life's extreme fragility
and remember its innocence
its original innocence
before you strike the first blow

Or perhaps never strike it
And let the light come through
the inner light of the canvas
the inner light of the models posed
in the life study
the inner light of everyone
Let it all come through
like a pentimento
the light that's been painted over
the life that's been painted over
so many times

Let it surge to the surface
the painted-over image
of primal life on earth

And when you've finished your painting
stand back astonished
stand back and observe
the life on earth that you've created
the lighted life on earth
that you've created
a new brave world

A New Brave World
CR

L AWRENCE FERLINGHETTI IS PROBABLY not a poet one would associate readily with a discussion of prayer. Ferlinghetti is one of the last living members of the Beat generation of poets who came of age in the 1950s. The Beats delighted in challenging the conventions of their day along with poetic tradition. Ferlinghetti wrote iconoclastic, irreverent poetry. When I was a senior in high school, a close friend lent me Ferlinghetti's collection, *A Coney Island of the Mind.* It was a dog-eared New Directions paperback to which she had lovingly imbued quasi-Scriptural meaning. My friend directed me to *Christ Climbed Down,* a poem in which Ferlinghetti imagines Christ's alienation as he encounters the crass commercialization of his birthday served up each year. In the closing image of the poem, Christ climbs down from his cross and steals away into some new Mary's womb. That image has remained with me all these years. I was drawn to Ferlinghetti's hipster vocabulary (Crazy, man!) because it so joyfully, angrily rebelled against the status quo. Understandably, the Beats weren't considered real poets in academia. They still aren't in some circles.

What a surprise then to encounter a much-mellowed Ferlinghetti some forty years later. *Instructions to Painters & Poets,* with its meditative, chantlike quality, could be considered one long prayer. If someone had covered up the name of the author, I might have guessed the poem was written by St. Francis of Assisi, not the cool old guy who showed up to read his work recently in Chicago wearing a bomber jacket, leather aviator cap, and goggles (evidently, the iconoclast still lives!). The Ferlinghetti penchant for repetition has not changed greatly. The devotion to improving the world, and the use of poetry toward that end, once an irritant to the gray-flannel world of the fifties, is still there, too. But *Instructions* is not the diatribe of rebellious youth. It is a rather wonderful visit with a man who has aged gracefully and has matured in experience and insight. Now in his eighties, he seems to be preparing for his life to end. It's as if he wants to leave behind a generous bequest of wisdom so that we might, ourselves, grow and mature.

The poem needs very little explanation, yet it is the kind that can be read time and again. I find something new with each reading. Ferlinghetti invites his readers to recognize that we are all painters and poets. He is a teacher who longs to impart the knowledge of a lifetime: "how to paint sunlight / on the face of life." The voice is calm, reassuring. All we have to do "is conceive of the whole world / and all humanity / as a kind of art work /. . . / an art project of the god of light."

Ferlinghetti's message has always been that art is for all of us, and that all of us are artists. In *Instructions,* he goes a step further. He asks us to accept his basic premise that all of humanity is a work of art. "And the first thing you have to do / is paint out postmodern painting." That line drew an appreciative laugh when Judy and I read the poem before a group from St. Xavier University in Chicago. The king of hip himself seemed to poke fun at his brother and sister artists who think art isn't great unless nobody understands it. "The next thing is to paint yourself / in your true colors / in primary colors." I imagined my Crayola crayons of childhood, their waxy reds, oranges, greens, and blues. These were our colors before we wore makeup, fashioned our personal masks, otherwise called adult sophistication. "Then paint your favorite people and animals." What a delightful exercise to stop and consider. I would select my daughter Rachel and son-in-law Greg. I would paint them sitting in rapt silence reading: she Virginia Woolf, he Ray Bradbury. Or I would paint them chatting as they collaborate on one of their thousand-piece jigsaw puzzles. Then I would pose my younger daughter, Meghan, an art student at Wellesley College. I would paint her, well, painting her own canvas. I would depict Judy simply smiling or gently wrinkling her brow as she listens attentively to one of her interview subjects. Finally, I would array all my pet dogs in a single painting, the two wonder-eyed mini dachshunds we now have, and all the others reaching back into memory. Now that I am a painter in my imagination, I'm able to see how it is done: "with [a] brush loaded with light." I know not to "fake it / because one false line leads to another."

Ferlinghetti suggests painting "on an autumn morning," against a brilliant palette of leaves. I will be the good student. Last weekend I visited my younger daughter, Meghan, in Boston. I worked on a new poem as the mid-October colors blazed in the forest surrounding the lake at the center of campus. Today I am back home in central Illinois, writing these words at a place called Funk's Grove. I am looking at an outdoor altar in a site called the "Chapel of Templed Trees." The central Illinois colors are every bit as dramatic as the cadmium yellow, ochre, and vermillion leaves of the New England autumn I observed last weekend.

This painting, however, is not all color and light. We must not forget to paint the "dark corners . . . / the hidden places and minds and hearts / which light never reaches." The rebel poet has not lost his edge or his ability to cut to the truth. There is room in this canvas for "the caves of ignorance and fear / the pits of despair / the sloughs of despond." The canvas of life would be incomplete without them. Each of us knows these dark regions. In my work, it means confronting the darkness of domestic violence, an evil hidden in plain sight within our communities. As a journalist, Judy has summoned the light to expose the shameful abuse of young people by clergy, the unjust wages paid to church workers, the devastating divisions among people of faith.

Ferlinghetti connects the painting of truth to the painting of the eyes. I am essentially a shy person. It is often difficult for me to make and sustain eye contact with others. If our eyes are the windows to our soul, it is risky business to offer such intimate knowledge. Yet, in my line of work as a Circuit Court judge, I've found that the best courtroom advocates are the ones who permit jurors to see in their eyes whatever is there to see. Whether they are arguing for a client or against a defendant, it is their *authentic* perspective, disclosed by the eyes, that persuades jurors that their words represent more than gamesmanship or shallow rhetoric. It may be hard to define, a fellow judge once told me, but you recognize it when you see it. Thus, Ferlinghetti exhorts us to paint those who lived their lives as bearers of light. "Paint their eyes." Paint the "light of sunlit laughter / the song of eyes / the song of birds in flight."

Here I stop to think of all the people who have been bearers of light in my life. My journey well might have taken a significantly different direction had Father Jim Stahl not looked me in the eye while I was in eighth grade and helped me build the confidence to lead our Catholic Youth Organization at Christ the King parish; if Father Joe Kelly had not reminded me of my essential worth during one of the most difficult crises in my life; if Sister Marilyn Ring hadn't offered words of understanding during my separation and divorce. Some of the light bearers were creatures, like my Sealyham terrier Alice, who stood by my side as I dealt with the upheaval of my parents' divorce. I was only five when that happened, and much of that year remains blanked out in memory, yet I remember Alice's luminous eyes. There were people with whom I worked, sometimes my subordinates, who possessed the courage to look me in the eye and tell me, with penetrating insistence, that I needed to shut up and listen. If they hadn't, my career might have turned out much differently. I have been blessed by the light in the eyes of so many genuine friends. As the hymn says, "how can I keep from singing" of their eyes, minds, and hearts?

Ferlinghetti ends his instructions with perhaps the most difficult task of all, self-portraiture. This requires a special technique. You must paint from the inside, he says. "Start with purity / with pure white." Look for the inner light. Let it surge to the surface. And when you've finished your painting, "stand back and observe / the life on earth that you've created / the lighted life on earth / . . . / a new brave world."

I want to thank this old radical for still trying to reinvent the world and the way we see ourselves in it. For forty years now, his poetry has made my world a little braver, and my soul a little newer.

Twenty More Poems to Nourish Your Soul

I F THE POEMS IN this book have touched you, please continue to explore the riches of poetry as sources of spiritual nourishment. You have many choices. Here are twenty more poems that we especially like:

Hope Lisel Mueller

One Art Elizabeth Bishop

Rowing Anne Sexton

Four Quartets T. S. Eliot

Work Mary Oliver

When Death Comes Mary Oliver

Pied Beauty Gerard Manley Hopkins

Eternal Poetry Carl Dennis

The Attic Marie Howe

Clearances Seamus Heaney

Poetry Pablo Neruda

Final Soliloquy of the Interior Paramour Wallace Stevens

Self-Portrait David Whyte

Recuerdo Edna St. Vincent Millay

Steps Frank O'Hara

Crossing Brooklyn Ferry Walt Whitman

Hope Emily Dickinson

To An Athlete Dying Young A. E. Houseman

The Paper Nautilus Marianne Moore

Archaeology Charles Wright

ACKNOWLEDGMENTS

"Poetry" from *ISLA NEGRA* by Pablo Neruda, translated by Alastair Reid, reprinted by permission of Farrar, Straus and Giroux, LLC.

"The Summer Day" From *House of Light* by Mary Oliver
Copyright © 1990 Mary Oliver
Reprinted by permission of Beacon Press, Boston

"The Layers," from *THE COLLECTED POEMS* by Stanley Kunitz. Copyright © 2000 by Stanley Kunitz. Used by permission of W. W. Norton & Company, Inc.

"Alive Together" reprinted by permission of Louisiana State University Press from *Alive Together: New and Selected Poems* by Lisel Mueller. Copyright © 1996 by Lisel Mueller.

"What the Living Do," from *WHAT THE LIVING DO* by Marie Howe. Copyright © 1997 by Marie Howe. Used by permission of W. W. Norton & Company, Inc.

"The God Who Loves You," from *PRACTICAL GODS* by Carl Dennis, copyright © 2001 by Carl Dennis. Used by permission of Viking Penguin, a division of Penguin Group (USA) Inc.

"To the Mistakes" by W. S. Merwin © 2001 by W. S. Merwin, reprinted with the permission of the Wylie Agency Inc.

"Twinings Orange Pekoe" by Judith Moffett from *Whinny Moor Crossing* by Judith Moffett (Princeton: Princeton University Press, 1984). Copyright © 1984 Judith Moffett. Reprinted by permission of the author.

"Aimless Love," copyright © 2002 by Billy Collins, "Poetry," copyright © 2002 by Billy Collins, from *NINE HORSES* by Billy Collins. Used by permission of Random House, Inc.

"The Greatest Grandeur" by Pattiann Rogers from *Song of the World Becoming: New and Collected Poems, 1981–2001* by Pattiann Rogers (Minneapolis: Milkweed Editions, 2001). Copyright © 2001 Pattiann Rogers. Reprinted by permission of the author.

"Kamehameha Drive-In, 25 Years Later" by Barbara Hamby from *The Alphabet of Desire* by Barbara Hamby (New York: New York University Press, 1999). Copyright © 1999 Barbara Hamby. Reprinted with permission of the author.

"Perennial" by Susan Hahn from *Mother in Summer* by Susan Hahn (Evanston: TriQuarterly Books/Northwestern University Press, 2002). Copyright © 2002 by Susan Hahn. Reprinted by permission of Northwestern University Press and the author.

"The Idea of Ancestry" and "Belly Song" are from *THE ESSENTIAL ETHERIDGE KNIGHT,* by Etheridge Knight, © 1986. Reprinted by permission of the University of Pittsburgh Press.

"Star Turn" from *APPALACHIA* by Charles Wright. Copyright © 1998 by Charles Wright. Reprinted by permission of Charles Wright and Farrar, Straus and Giroux, LLC.

"The Panther" by Rainer Maria Rilke, translated by C. F. MacIntyre, from *Selected Poems: Bilingual Edition* by Rainer Maria Rilke (Berkeley, CA: University of California Press, 2001), originally published as *Rainer Maria Rilke: Fifty Selected Poems* by Rainer Maria Rilke (Berkeley, CA: University of California Press, 1940). Copyright © 1940 C. F. MacIntyre. Reprinted with permission of University of California Press.

"The Hammock" by Li-Young Lee from *Book of My Nights.* Copyright © 2001 by Li-Young Lee. Reprinted with the permission of BOA Editions, Ltd., www.BOAEditions.org.

"Instructions to Painters & Poets" by Lawrence Ferlinghetti, from *HOW TO PAINT SUNLIGHT,* copyright © 2001 by Lawrence Ferlinghetti. Reprinted by permission of New Directions Publishing Corp.
SALES TERRITORY: U.S./Canadian rights only.

About the Authors

JUDITH VALENTE is an on-air correspondent for the national PBS program *Religion & Ethics NewsWeekly.* She regularly interviews poets on WBEZ Chicago Public Radio. She worked previously as a staff writer for the *Washington Post* and the *Wall Street Journal,* where she was a finalist for the Pulitzer Prize, and as a special writer for *People* magazine. Her chapbook, *Inventing an Alphabet,* was selected by Mary Oliver for the 2005 Aldrich Poetry Prize. Her poems have appeared in the literary journals *TriQuarterly, Folio, RHINO, The Rambler* and *After Hours.* She received an Illinois Arts Council poetry award in 2003 for her poem *Green* and an Illinois Arts Council grant in 2005. She holds a bachelor's degree in English from St. Peter's College in Jersey City, New Jersey, and a master's of fine arts in creative writing from the School of the Art Institute of Chicago.

CHARLES REYNARD is a judge of the Eleventh Judicial Circuit in Central Illinois. He was State's Attorney of McLean County, Illinois, from 1987 to 2002. Mr. Reynard also worked as an assistant public defender and was a defense attorney in private practice for ten years. He is a nationally recognized expert on the prosecution of sexual assault and child sex abuse cases. The recipient of numerous civic awards, he has lectured on criminal justice topics throughout the United

States and in Russia and Nigeria. He is a founder of the Children's Advocacy Center in McLean County, Illinois, and served as chairman of the Continuing Legal Education for Illinois Prosecutors Committee and on the Illinois Violence Prevention Authority. Mr. Reynard holds a bachelor's degree in English from St. Joseph's College in Indiana and a Juris Doctor degree from Loyola University Chicago School of Law. His poems have appeared in the anthology *Illinois Poets: Where We Live* and the Chicago literary journal *After Hours*. He was a 2003 finalist for the Gwendolyn Brooks award for emerging poets and a 2004 semifinalist for the Emily Dickinson award from Universities West Press.

A Special Invitation

Loyola Press invites you to become one of our Loyola Press Advisors! Join our unique online community of people willing to share with us their thoughts and ideas about Catholic life and faith. By sharing your perspective, you will help us improve our books and serve the greater Catholic community.

From time to time, registered advisors are invited to participate in online surveys and discussion groups. Most surveys will take less than ten minutes to complete. Loyola Press will recognize your time and efforts with gift certificates and prizes. Your personal information will be held in strict confidence. Your participation will be for research purposes only, and at no time will we try to sell you anything.

Please consider this opportunity to help Loyola Press improve our products and better serve you and the Catholic community. To learn more or to join, visit our Web site at **www.Spirited Talk.org** and register today.

—The Loyola Press Advisory Team